FLOWERS

Gardeners'
World

FLOWERS

TOBY BUCKLAND

Photography by Jason Ingram

PLANNING AND PLANTING FOR CONTINUOUS COLOUR

635.9

Contents

Introduction   7
Part 1 Creating Your flower garden   10

Part 2 The Flower Gardens at Greenacre   40
1 | The Twilight Garden   42
2 | The Bee Border   60
3 | The Scented Front Garden   76
4 | The Bank   92
5 | The Woodland Garden   104
6 | The Bedding Borders   124
7 | The Modern Prairie Border   140
8 | The Coastal Garden   156
9 | The Seed-Packet Meadows   170
10 | The Cut Flower Garden   182
11 | The Exotic Garden   202

Index   220
Ackowledgements   224

Introduction

Whenever I meet gardeners, the first thing most people ask is 'What can I grow to make my garden more colourful?' Well, this book is the answer to that question. All of the 200-plus plants within this book grow at Greenacre, the BBC Gardeners' World HQ, so they must have on-screen presence for much of the year. I've grown them all so I know they are tried-and-tested performers.

This book is all about how to have a garden brimming with blooms. It identifies the best flowers for a variety of situations and schemes, and explains how to combine, tend and enjoy them so your borders have year-round sparkle. No matter where you garden there are flowers here for you. Some thrive in the most difficult situations such as the shade under trees, or on thin soils in baking sun. Others are brilliant for giving your garden a stylish look, be it exotic, romantic or modern.

I've made sure to include flowers for every month of the year, some long-serving ones for a continuity of colour and others that bloom in a short but magnificent flush. As well as beauty, many of my selections are useful too, filling the air with fragrance, providing pollen and nectar for bees or grown to fill vases in your house.

It's impossible for me to pick a favourite flower because each one is perfect in its moment, as welcome as the last. The colour, scent and sheer loveliness of the petals cheers up the bad times and help to celebrate the good. But that's only part of the pleasure. It's the planting, tending and all that goes with it that make flowers such a joy.

The Greenacre Map

The plan of the Greenacre garden (not to scale) showing the flower gardens featured in this book, plus the other gardens that make up the site.

The Bank

Joe's Garden

Mediterranean Garden

N

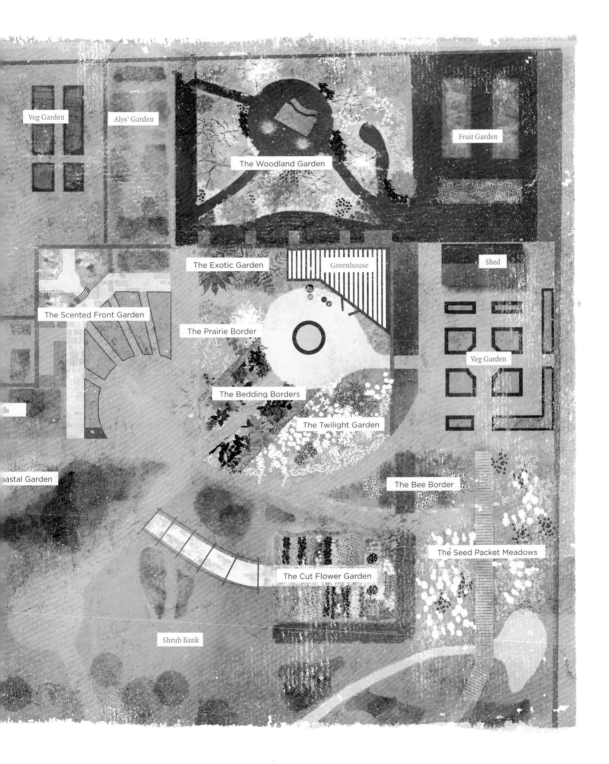

Veg Garden

Alys' Garden

Fruit Garden

The Woodland Garden

The Exotic Garden

Greenhouse

Shed

The Scented Front Garden

The Prairie Border

Veg Garden

The Bedding Borders

The Twilight Garden

...ds

...astal Garden

The Bee Border

The Seed Packet Meadows

The Cut Flower Garden

Shrub Bank

1 | CREATING YOUR FLOWER GARDEN

Brightening up the Coastal Garden with cuttings-grown *Lampranthus*.

Getting started

This book is divided into eleven chapters, each one representing a different garden at Greenacre with a selection of the major players needed to create the look. Do refer to the panel on the first page of each chapter to check that you can give the plants the right conditions and that their maintenance implications are right for you. Apart from a few exceptions – the Bank, Coastal Garden and Woodland – all of the flowers are happy in average garden soil that is neither extremely alkaline or acidic, nor waterlogged. Take it from me, when we first arrived Greenacre's soil was no picnic, in a former life it was rugby pitch compacted by years of scrums and line-outs and a tricky acidic sandy-loam. But by steadily improving it with well-rotted manure and mushroom compost we now have lovely, crumbly beds that are moist, aerated and filled with the nutrients required for healthy growth.

Use the illustrations to understand how the border is balanced by quantities and groupings of plants. The idea is that you can select as many or as few plants and styles as you like to suit your garden. Just a few individual flowers or combinations could brighten up an already established border, or you could create a whole new border or several borders from scratch.

Understanding flowers

Perennials, annuals and biennials
Most of the flowers in this book are perennials – flowers which live three years or more in the UK, usually dying down to the ground in winter and reappearing in spring. Annuals germinate from seed, flower and die in the same year, while biennials live through their cycle over two, flowering in their second year.

Flowering types
Most flowers bloom for a few weeks in one season only, though mostly in summer. Summer flowers can be divided into early, mid and late-summer flowering. Combining a good spread of flowers with different flowering times rather than focussing on single, long-flowering plants, creates an ever-changing tapestry of colour. Some plants can be induced to bloom more prolifically or repeatedly by judicious pruning and deadheading.

Shapes
Flowers belong in botanical families, distinguished by the arrangement of their flower parts and petals, including umbels (with an umbrella shape), daisies, spikes and racemes. Planting large

clumps of contrasting shapes, for example daisies adjacent to umbels or globes, appeals to the eye, creating an impression of depth and colour.

Hardiness

Flowers span the spectrum from very hardy (won't die in sub-zero temperatures) to very tender (will keel over with the first frost). The extremes hold true in gardens across the UK, it is the plants inbetween that vary – the half-hardies and semi-tenders which can be coaxed to live through milder winters or where frosts are less penetrating, such as coastal or urban locations. Keeping plants going from year to year, whether through cuttings or protection from the elements, is all part of the skill and fun of being a gardener.

Improving your colour quota

Having a garden that looks colourful for most of the year isn't just about what you grow, but also how you grow it. Perennial flowers are rarely used on their own in a border due to the fact that most die down in winter, leaving nothing to see until spring returns. They are better planted with a complement of shrubs or ornamental grasses along with trees and hedges.

Think not only horizontally, but also vertically, and clothe fences, walls as well as shrubs and trees with flowering climbers to bring colour up to eye-level where you really notice it. Construct pergolas, obelisks, arbours and arches to grow climbers up and to use as props for shrub roses and wall shrubs. Attach windowboxes to ledges and huddle containers together in groups for the largest impact. Colonise gaps in paving and dry stone and brickwork walls (see page 56) to soften hard surfaces and create colour links between borders and the hard landscape.

Take time to understand the conditions in your garden and if plants fail in one area, try and work out why – is it too dry? too wet? too shady? – and discover the range of plants that will succeed.

Pulmonaria 'Blue Ensign' flowers in the depths of winter.

Dahlia 'Magenta Star'.

Try also to look beyond the conditions your garden already provides and create microclimates to extend the range of flowers you can grow. Build raised beds for plants which need well-drained conditions, or put up fences and spade manure into borders to create sheltered spots for hungry large-leaved exotics. Consider making space for a greenhouse, one of the best investments you can make if you want to extend the seasons.

Flowers unleash your creative side, particularly when you have to marry interesting combinations and colour-schemes. Simply by juxtaposing one flower colour against another can make a garden look more exciting and vibrant. Use the illustrated plans of each garden to discover which flowers I find make good neighbours and try out new mixtures and blends of your own.

When you think you can't fit another plant in your garden, look to bulbs. These papery packages are the best way to pack in more colour, requiring so little space they can be planted underneath the crown of existing perennials and add both another layer of colour through your flowers, and a prolonged season that extends either side of summer, from late winter right into autumn.

Preparing your site

Soil types
Soils can be divided into five different types – clay, sandy, chalky, loam and silty. This describes their composition and texture and also suggests their properties, for example moist or well-

drained. Soils are often a mixture of more than one type. At Greenacre we have sandy-clay soil. Soils also have a pH and can be neutral, acidic or alkaline. Many plants will happily grow in a range of pH soils, though some, notably rhododendrons and azaleas, suffer in alkaline soils.

Nirvana for plants is what's confusingly called a 'moist but well-drained soil' which means there is enough moisture for the plant not to wilt in summer, but not so much for it to get waterlogged. Loam, which is a mixture of sand, clay and well-rotted organic matter, is naturally like this, while clays and silts, which have closely packed particles, tend to dry out in summer and sit wet in winter. Sandy soil – also described as 'light' or 'free-draining' – tends to be dry and low in nutrients as the goodness washes away with rain.

Improving your soil

The good news is that without the need for a degree in soil science, you can be safe in the knowledge that improving your soil – whatever its type – will make it more conducive to growing plants. Ways to improve soil include annual mulching and digging in a spadeful or two of home-made compost whenever you plant anything, modifying what you use depending on what you're planting – adding well-rotted manure is ideal for hungry, fast-growing exotics and roses; leafmould is perfect for creating woodsy soil for woodlanders; and mushroom compost, which alleviates acidity, is good for wallflowers. The only soils you don't need to keep improving with compost are meadowland and parts of schemes like the Bank or Cut Flower gardens which are sown with annuals, which tend to make leaf at the expense of flowers in rich soil. Improving your soil isn't a one-off job. Mulching in spring and autumn adds organic matter which worms pull down into the soil, improving the texture and fertility. Never miss the opportunity to add more when planting, lifting and dividing or moving plants, too.

Plants are sometimes described as preferring a particular type of soil, for example 'fertile' or 'rich' soil, 'humus-rich' and 'improved', or 'free-draining'. In these cases, if your soil is either extremely light or very heavy, another choice would probably be more suitable, although improving the soil will still help.

Aspect

Position is another factor to take into consideration. Plants may prefer a sheltered spot, part-shade or full sun, for example. Shelter suggests a plant hates strong buffeting winds or tends not to flower well in exposed situations, so try to provide a spot which is warm and clement such as an enclosed garden or suntrapped site, or perhaps the base of a south-facing wall. Sun and shade are all defined by degrees. South and west-facing gardens are in full sun, though the addition of trees and building may throw the garden or a particular border into shade for part of the day (hence part shade). North and east-facing aspects tend to be shadier and colder due to the prevailing wind and frosts may linger here in winter. If you are unsure as to aspect simply note whee the sun rises and falls throughout the day, remembering that the sun rises in the east and sets in the west.

Successful planting

If you're creating an entirely new border, set out all the plants first so you can get an idea of spacing. Position plants so that their eventual spread just touches – this means if you have two plants with 60cm spread that's how far apart you position them. If you are planting things with different spreads, position half the width of their eventual spread away from the maximum spread of its neighbour. It doesn't have to be a job you need to agonise over, as flowers tend to fill the space they're given, spreading over time and you can always move them or fill any large gaps with fast-growing but short-lived annuals. Planting heights and spreads in this book, and indeed nursery catalogues, are approximate and dependent on the quality of the growing conditions. The more light, food and shelter a plant gets the larger it grows.

Chrysanthemum 'Beppie Red'.

Where you are adding just one or two plants to an established border, use sticks to hold back neighbours while working, and trim back overbearing plants to allow light into the newbies and give them a fighting chance.

Water new plants thoroughly before putting them in the ground. If they're very dry, or you have a few to plant, stick them in a water-filled barrow to soak for half an hour. If new introductions are planted dry, they won't have a reserve of moisture to keep them going while they establish their roots.

If you buy container-grown roses and herbaceous plants in spring, there's a good chance some compost will fall away as you knock them from their pots as nurseries tend to pot them up at this time of year. Don't be alarmed, just get them into the soil quickly, adding compost to the planting hole first, and gently brush earth over the bare roots. Conversely, towards the end of summer roots may be verging on pot-bound, spiralling around the inside of the plastic pot and emerging from the drainage holes. Waste no time getting them in the ground after buying and, if there is a delay, remember to water them regularly. Be sure to fan out the roots of pot-bound plants when planting, or they may waste time corkscrewing around in the soil for longer.

Attractive seedheads extend
a plant's season of interest,
and you can collect the seeds
for free flowers next year.

Give bare-root plants a good start

The traditional way to plant roses is as bare-roots, and many perennials and shrubs are available pot-free like this for planting in the dormant season. Dig a hole wide enough to accommodate the roots of the plant at the depth at which the plant was previously planted (you can see the mark on the stem. Roses and clematis need a hole a hands-width deeper.) Trim back any damaged roots to healthy growth (1) and add some mycorrhizae (see below) to the hole (2). Place a pole across the hole to make sure the plant is sitting at the correct depth and spread out the roots on the earth (3). Backfill the soil, breaking up clods with your fingers and crumbling the earth around the plant's roots. Firm in small plants with fingers or knuckles, and use the flat of your foot for larger specimens (anything grown in a 2-litre pot or bigger). Once planted, trim back the shoots to the first healthy bud (4). On slopes or ground prone to drying out, ridge up the soil into a crater around the roots to create a reservoir and prevent runoff.

Mycorrhizae is a fungus naturally found in soil with which plants share a symbiotic relationship. The fungi act as an extension of the plant's roots, gathering minerals and food. It as a proven way of helping hungry plants establish on tricky soils. It is available as a gel for dipping rootballs into or as a granule, for sprinkling onto wet roots. It has to be in contact with roots to work.

Dahlia 'Rothesay Reveller'.

Graceful Tulip 'White Triumphator',
one of the freshest whites.

Tulip 'Ballerina' flowers in late April.

Maintaining a flower garden

Watering

After investing time and money in creating a new border, you need to look after it. Watering is probably the most important thing to keep on top of in the first year after planting, as roots are still small and establishing. You may need to water throughout the year, not just in the summer when it is obviously hot and dry. For example, a couple of weeks of dry, windy weather in late spring or autumn can desiccate both new and established plants. Watch out for suffering plants and try not to let soil dry out.

Water properly, soaking the soil to at least 10cm deep (check by digging down with a trowel). Use whatever watering method you find the easiest – can, sprinkler or hose etc – and if possible do it in the evening, as there's less chance of moisture evaporating. It's most efficient to water by hand, whether using a can or a hosepipe, directing the flow directly to the plants' roots where it's needed and isn't wasted.

Weeding

Keep on top of annual weeds by hoeing bare soil in spring and summer, slicing the roots from the shoots and leaving them on the surface to dry out. This is a job best done on a sunny day as you get a guaranteed kill. I enjoy hoeing and my weapon of choice is the Dutch hoe. I prefer a stout wooden handle as the weight helps push the blade through the soil. For best results, work backwards, obliterating footprints as you go, and slide the blade back and forth through the top centimetre of soil. On our sandy soil the hoe blades are self-sharpening but on a clay or silt, invest in a file to sharpen it from time to time.

It's best to pull large and perennial weeds by hand after rain. Time it right, just after the rain has finished and the ground is starting to dry, and even deep-rooted docks and dandelions will slide from the soil intact. Unfortunately you'll need to be heavier handed when eradicating pernicious spreading weeds like couch grass and the white flowered twinning bindweed. Dig out what you can little and often, and if there's space between plants lay paper over the soil and cover with mulch for the growing season to finish off any survivors. Alternatively use the weedkiller glyphosate which, if used repeatedly, will eventually kill both roots and shoots. It's not as environment-friendly as other methods and you have to avoid the foliage of the flowers you want to keep, otherwise you'll kill them too.

Of course, all gardeners have to tolerate a certain amount of weeds, but the key is to never allow one to go to seed. As soon as they raise their faces above the parapet of blooms, it's off with their heads.

Erigeron karvinskianus self-seeds in cracks in walls and paving.

Feeding and improving soil

At Greenacre, we believe in feeding the soil not the plants, so the bulk of our fertilising is done when new borders are created. However, extra feeding is always necessary in some circumstances, particularly with hungry plants like dahlias, clematis and roses, and displays of lush exotics and bedding. Here's the lowdown on the feeds we use at Greenacre:

Balanced fertiliser

We apply the balanced fertiliser fish, blood and bone to permanent residents (roses and clematis etc) in spring. This helps them to produce plenty of flower-bearing stems and helps them be robust and disease-free. We apply another dose in wet summers to ensure the continually growing displays don't run out of steam.

High-nitrogen

If plants have lack-lustre leaves, spindly stems and look like they need a boost, they're probably lacking in nitrogen. Chicken manure is a high-nitrogen feed, which benefits leafy growth and is good for greening up palms and making exotics like bananas, cannas and colocasia soar. The different brands vary, and some are smellier than others, so choose with your nose – and don't use in a small front garden.

High-potash

Use a high-potash feed (a liquid tomato fertiliser is ideal) on bedding flowers and to toughen up tender flowers before the arrival of the winter cold. Apply it to the ground as a dilute liquid feed every couple of weeks until the end of September. It's also the one to use to preserve the colour of purple-leaved plants (high-nitrogen chicken manure will turn them green). To save the cash we make our own high-potash feed from crushed comfrey leaves and water.

Tonics and trace elements

These give plants a lift and increase the lustre of foliage without causing rapid growth. Unlike artificial fertilisers they can be applied late in the growing season without the risk of promoting soft foliage that's easily scorched by frost. Seaweed foliar feed is one of the best you can use.

'Rubinstern', one of the most reliable echinacea.

As soon as plants go to seed they stop producing blooms so deadheading will keep plants flowering for longer.

Deadheading and cutting back

The key to prolonging the performance of repeat-flowering plants is to remove spent blooms as they go over. Different plants are deadheaded in different ways but, in essence, you're aiming to do two things: avoid accidentally taking off upcoming buds and remove as much spent flower stalk as possible.

It's not an exact science, but aim to snip off the flower and the stalk it sits on, back to nearest leaves. With single-headed perennials that send up flower stalks from a basal crown of leaves, like a red hot poker, it's obvious you cut it off at the base close to the crown. Those that flower atop leafy stems, such as salvia, and helenium, form sprays of buds, meaning you just take off the individuals as they go over, removing the flower stalk back to the nearest main stem. It's the same with roses, but when a whole cluster has gone over, trim back the spent stem not to the first but the second bud below the blooms as it'll grow more strongly and because the wood is thicker hold the flowers more upright. Like all gardening jobs, the more you do it the quicker and more confident you get.

Removing dead-heads from flowers that bloom once, bulbs are a good example, won't encourage a second flush but it does concentrate the energy from the leaves into bulking up the bulbs so it puts on an even bigger show next year. It also prevents them looking straggly and untidy, particularly those with showy flowers like peonies.

With large areas of bedding or meadow annuals, keeping on top of deadheading is a full-time job that few people have time for. As a result, it's best to ruthlessly blitz these areas every few weeks snipping back to healthy leaves and watering and feeding with a high-potash fertiliser. The display will bounce back in no time at all. Similarly, don't muck about with plants that age terribly after flowering, including cranesbill geraniums, alchemillla, oriental poppies and catmint. These can all be brutally cut back to their crown and, once watered and fed, will produce fresh growth and often a second, smaller flush of flowers.

Pruning lavender

Prune lavender after flowering finishes in late August with sheers or secateurs. Remove the spent flowerspikes and top 5cm of leafy growth.

Give it another trim in spring to keep it nice and bushy.

Elegant *Gladiolus nanus*
need no staking.

Verbascum, stipa and *phormium* in the Coastal Garden.

Yellow pompoms of cotton lavender.

Staking

It's best to stake plants before they reach full height. This way it can be done unobtrusively and the stakes disappear from sight as plants grow. Also, once plants have toppled it's very difficult to get them upright again and look natural.

I like to stake with hazel, willow and twiggy peasticks as they blend in. I tend to buy a job lot from a local tree surgeon in winter in readiness for spring staking. It's worth calling local tree surgeons to see if they have anything, and you can also check out www.coppice-products.co.uk for a directory of coppice workers in your area who often have cut sticks ideal for staking. Of course, this style isn't for everyone and there are several different ways to successfully stake plants.

Bamboo canes and twine (1) are ideal for tall, back-of-the-border delphiniums and asters – anything that's big and demands a heavy-duty support. Push three to five canes into the ground so they are two-thirds the height of the clump in a ring around the crown. Loop twine around the tops of the canes, gathering all of the central stems together but leaving a few outside of the twine. Tie these loosely to the canes, disguising your work and creating a natural look. You can also make attractive wigwams for sweet peas (4).

A criss-cross of twine across entire borders is good for keeping long runs of plants from sprawling over paths. Push canes into the ground at the front and back of borders and weave twine diagonally between them to create a supporting net. This method also works well for tall bedding like nicotiana and as a corral in border

Plastic covered wire stakes are best installed in March and April so foliage grows up to hide them – any later and they are hard to place.

Peasticks (2) make great rescue props. Sharpen their ends to make it easier to push them into dry soil. Buy them fresh every year.

Criss-cross domes create a natural, airy look for plants like asters and peonies. Use twiggy stems and push them into the ground to make a ring around plants. Snap over and bind tops together to create a dome-shaped mesh that stems will grow up through, and which is also a useful support for netting to keep off birds.

Posts and loops (3) are ideal for crops like cut flowers. Hammer a post into the ground at the end of rows and encircle the crop with a long loop of twine tied at each end.

Plant *Allium sphaerocephalon* to grow through lavender.

Lifting and dividing

Herbaceous perennials grow in a spreading fashion, sending out roots from around the plant to colonise new, fertile ground. After two to three years, they may have moved a few feet from where you planted them, or grown outwards in a concentric ring, leaving a dead patch in the centre. If this is the case, it's time to lift plants, roots and all, split them up into smaller clumps and replant. You can put the original back into position and replant with more to enlarge drifts, or pot up spares to use in other areas of your garden at a later date.

Getting the timing right is key when dividing or moving plants. With plants that flower before July, divide in autumn to give them time to bulk up and provide a good show next year. With tender flowers and those that appear from high summer onwards, divide in spring. Divide springflowering plants in the summer.

Dividing plants isn't difficult, but you do need to take care. Start by digging up the plant with a spade and lifting it clear of the soil with a fork – ensure as many roots are intact as possible. Look at the roots to ascertain the best method of division – some are woody, others are fleshy or fibrous, while others divide into rosettes or offsets and can be gently teased apart by hand. It's always worth trying to tear roots either by hand or with a fork as you inevitably keep more of the root intact. However, for those with thick woody or fleshy roots – hostas and bamboo spring to mind – use a knife, saw or spade to chop through them. For anything else, use two back-to-back forks to prize plants apart (see page 155).

Discard old, tired bits at the centre of the plant and retain just healthy sections for replanting. Keep clumps a minimum of half the size of the blade of a spade so they re-establish and flower well. Always take the opportunity to freshen up the planting hole with more compost and a sprinkle of bonemeal when replanting.

Squirrel tail grass.

Greenacre's friendly robin
– we call him Dwayne!

Troubleshooting

I've covered specific vectors of individual plants in the maintenance regime of each chapter, but it's worth mentioning how we tackle the problems that are common to all gardens at Greenacre:

Aphids

It is not always possible to stop aphid numbers getting out of hand, particularly in wet springs, as the moisture fuels soft new growth which aphids love. My attitude to controlling aphids requires certain brinkmanship. If they're sprayed too early with contact insecticide their natural predators (ladybirds, spiders and lacewings) will also be killed, making the aphid damage even worse. So I tend to leave them, and if the damage becomes overly apparent, or the plant's life is at risk, I spray with a plant invigorator. This is new type of foliar feed that boosts plant health and glues aphids to the spot so they can't feed. It also works on sap-sucking insects including scale, whitefly, greenfly and spider mite. Because it is a mechanical method of killing, as opposed to a poison or nerve toxin, it doesn't get into the food chain, and doesn't harm natural predators.

Birds

In the early days crows were our main problem at Greenacre. They were constantly pulling out new plants and pecking seedlings. The solution has been to make the garden more enclosed, with internal hedges, screens and banks of shrubs – if crows don't have a good line of sight to spot predators coming, they're less likely to do damage. Netting supported on willow hoops seems to keep pigeons off newly sown areas, although it doesn't deter clever crows – they weigh down the netting by dropping stones on it to get to seed. One positive effect of deterring the crows has been burgeoning numbers of hedgerow birds. Bluetits, robins and blackbirds have made the garden their home and started to patrol, eating caterpillars, aphids and slugs.

Caterpillars

The odd caterpillar does very little harm, so I leave tend to leave them unless they're on a prized plant when I pick them off and put them on the bird table. Where damage is severe (leaves reduced to a skeleton of veins) the culprit is usually sawfly larvae. They look like small green caterpillars and feed on just one type of flower, so they won't spread and devour your whole garden. At the early stages of infestation pick off by hand or prune away affected leaves and bury in them in your compost heap. When attacks are severe you have two choices: either spray with a contact insecticide or, as we do at Greenacre, use a natural nematode spray to kill them off.

Earwigs

Earwigs spoil flowers of dahlias, chrysanths and clematis, coming out at night to chew on petals. Look out for them holed-up in nearby wall or fence crevices by day or catch them in straw-filled pots upturned on bamboo canes in the border. At Greenacre we put these omnivores on the compost heap, as they do eat aphids and break down plant material.

Harlequin ladybirds

When harlequin ladybirds first arrived on these shores from America there was a great deal written in the press about how they would kill off our native species. However, harlequin ladybirds have mated with the native population and are now here in such number that experts believe it's impossible to get rid of them. Many also look like natives, so telling them apart is difficult to do and it is not recommended to kill them. The only positive is that mites which parasitise our native ladybirds now prey on harlequins, so numbers should be kept in balance.

Mammals

Rabbits and deer can be a real problem in the countryside, and the only way to deal with them effectively is to erect wire fences to keep them out. Plant a hedge (box or privet for rabbits, beech or hornbeam for deer) close to the fence line so it hides the wire and your garden doesn't end up looking like a prison camp. In urban areas foxes, and more often cats, are the problem, scraping and using newly prepared beds as a loo. Again, physical barriers are the way to stop this. Sprigs of holly laid on the soil make an effective deterrent as do cheap wooden barbeque skewers – push them into the earth to form a grid, point side down and spaced 15cm apart.

No flowers

If flowers refuse to bloom there are a number of possible problems, but the most likely is immaturity. Perennials may take a year to bulk up before flowering. The other is some deficiency, either a sun-lover lacking sun, a hungry plant lacking nutrients or a lack of water when the plant was developing flower-buds. Overfeeding with nitrogenous feeds will make foliage at the expense of petals, use high-potash feeds for flowers.

Slugs and snails

Left to their own devices slugs and snails eat almost everything so it's vital to campaign against them. Concentrate your efforts during periods of prolonged wet by scattering wildlife-friendly slug pellets through borders and by using biological nematode slug killers. Nematodes are microscopic worms, invisible to the naked eye, that infect slugs with a natural bacteria that kills them off. It sounds gruesome but, like encouraging birds to eat caterpillars and slugs, it is a way of tipping the balance of nature in your flowers' favour. Once numbers are under control, use beer traps – margarine tubs with a hole cut in the side that slugs (but not predatory beetles) can access, half-filled with beer. The slugs sniff out the sugary brew and drown in the drink. Also, scatter organic slug pellets that contain ferric phosphate around the feet of plants after wet weather.

Vine weevils

If you notice pot plants wilt when the compost is moist the chances are vine weevils are eating the roots. Attacks occur in spring and early autumn when the majority of the white, 1cm brown-headed grubs hatch and start feeding. Mail-order nematode drenches are the way to prevent and deal with established populations. Water on to the compost and the microscopic predatory nematodes will hunt and kill them for you. Attacks are most common in peat-based compost, less so in soil based John Inness as the gritty texture makes it harder for the grubs to move about.

Perfect early-summer partners - *Astrantia* 'Hadspen Blood' and *Allium* 'Globemaster'.

Pulmonaria provides nectar for newly-woken bees in late winter.

Dahlia 'Twynings After Eight' has chocolate-coloured leaves and stem.

Coreopsis tinctonia and *Ammi majus* in the Seed-Packet Meadow.

2 | THE FLOWER GARDENS AT GREENACRE

Globes of *Stipitatum* 'Mount Everest' float above fragrant sweet rocket.

1 THE TWILIGHT GARDEN

The Twilight Garden was the first to be created at Greenacre because it has a high-profile filming position near the greenhouse. It comprises three planting areas circling a gravel area and a raised pond, totals roughly 40 square metres and is protected by south- and west-facing walls. The walls and gravel create a sheltered microclimate that holds the heat of the day – and fragrance from the flowers – long into the night. It's a pleasant place to sit and dream away a summer evening.

The plants are a mix of shrubs, roses, perennials and annuals, which are all predominantly shades of white and silver. While a white garden looks stunning by day, it really comes to life in the evening when flowers and leaves glow with an ethereal light, even showing up after dark when lit by the moon. To set off the white and silver, I have used a smattering of purple-leaved shrubs and perennials.

There's more to a white garden than just its good looks, though. Many white flowers have a sumptuous evening fragrance and have evolved to attract pollinating moths which, thanks to their strong sense of smell, are drawn to the nectar. Moths are valuable in a garden's eco-system, and seeking them out to identifying their shapes and forms is a fascinating pastime (see page 59). They're also suffering from habitat loss and, according to figures from Butterfly Conservation, numbers have dropped by a third since 1968. As a result, anything gardeners can do to attract moths should be encouraged, and planting a twilight garden is a very good start.

In a nutshell: *this is a stylish collection of white and scented plants. It includes shrubs, roses and perennials and is designed to look at its best in the evening*

Suited to: *this scheme's for you if you like cool colours and scent*

Ideal location: *you need a sheltered, sunny and enclosed area, preferably next to your patio or seating area. Any ordinary, non-boggy soil will do*

Space needed: *a minimum of six square metres is ideal*

Maintenance rating: *high. You'll need to tend this scheme little and often*

Eco credentials: *excellent. Many of the plants in this scheme are attractive to moths and butterflies, both of which are in decline*

Borders planted with white alliums and tulips.

White snapdragon, alyssum and *Cosmos* 'Purity' used as fillers around edges.

1: *Stachys byzantia*
2: *Rosa* Kew Gardens (Ausfence)
3: *Cleome hassleriana* 'Helen Campbell'
4: *Antirrhinum majus* 'Royal Bride'
5: *Sambucus nigra* f. porphyrophylla 'Eva'
6: *Hesperis matronalis*
7: *Anemone* x *hybrida* 'Honorine Jobert'
8: *Lychnis coronaria* 'Alba'
9: *Lilium regale*
10: *Dahlia* 'Joe Swift'
11: *Digitalis purpurea* 'Pam's Choice'
12: *Dahlia* 'Twyning's After Eight'
13: *Griselinia* hedge
14: *Passiflora caerulea*
15: *Nicotiana sylvestris*
16: *Artemisia* 'Powis Castle'
17: *Lavandula stoechas*
18: *Eryngium bourgatii* 'Picos Amethyst'
19: *Astelia chathamica*
20: *Cynara cardunculus*

N

Twilight Garden elements

White

You needn't be strict about only using Hollywood-teeth-white plants. Blush pinks, pale greens and off-whites all work and create a rich tapestry when combined. Creams and pale yellows need selecting carefully though, as some tones can turn a milk-white scheme sour. Also be wary of white flowers that have vivid, contrasting centres.

Depth

There's a risk that a mass of white flowers will look monotonous and a bit flat. To avoid this, and to bring depth to a scheme, add contrasting evergreens with green, purple or silver foliage. This enhances the sparkle of pale blooms.

Shelter

A sheltered location is essential, as it will harbour scent, adds to the sense of calm, and encourages moths and butterflies to settle. If you don't have a sheltered spot, create one with fence panels, large plants or hedges.

Constant Colour

Use annuals, biennials and bulbs to extend the flowering season. Spring-flowering bulbs, like white daffodils and tulips, kick-start the colour early in the year, followed by foxgloves, alliums and sweet rocket for early summer colour. Perennials should pick up the baton for the rest of the year.

Evening-scented *nicotiana* sways above a foam of cosmos and snapdragons.

My plant choices

It never fails to amaze me how many different shades of white flower exist. You've got glossy dahlias, powdery nicotiana, bone-white cosmos and a whole variety of creams, off-whites, blush-pinks and greens to choose from. However, a collection of pale flowers won't create a white border as most are borne on green-leaved plants. For that you need contrast, so make sure you include silver-leaved evergreens, which will add sparkle when there are few flowers about, and dark-leaved plants, such as Sambucus 'Eva', as a backdrop to make the whites glow. If you match whites you create a cleaner, more formal look, whereas a mixture of whites looks warmer and more natural.

Bulbs are brilliant because they have strong eye-catching shapes and extend the seasons. We've chosen ours in varying heights and flowering times for a succession of interest, growing through and around the evergreens and perennials. Scented annuals such as alyssum draw in wildlife and form useful ground cover, even in semi-shade, from spring to late summer.

Annuals and Biennials
Sow from seed and use to fill gaps and to produce a constant display.

Cleome hassleriana
'Helen Campbell' (AGM)
Flowers: JUNE–JULY
Height/spread: 1.5M X 60CM
This frost-tender annual provides an elegant froth of white flowers. Its long, spidery stamens protrude from the large, scented, white blooms, giving them a spidery appearance. Grow in light, fertile, preferably sandy and free-draining soil in full sun. Good for moths.

Antirrhinum majus 'Royal Bride' (AGM)
Flowers: JUNE–SEPTEMBER
Height/spread: 80CM X 50CM
This is a scented white snapdragon which makes a muscular summer gap filler. It dies back gracefully in autumn. Deadhead throughout the summer.

Cosmos bipinnatus 'Purity'

Flowers: JUNE–OCTOBER
Height/spread: 1M X 60CM
An easy border annual that flourishes in full sun from midsummer onwards. Its large, saucer-shaped flowers are offset by masses of mid-green, feathery foliage. Grow in moist but well-drained soil. Regular dead-heading encourages continual flowering.

Digitalis purpurea
'Pam's Choice'

Flowers: MAY–JUNE
Height/spread: 1.2M X 50CM

How's this for a glow-in-the-dark foxglove? Its stout, strong spires of creamy-white flowers have throats splashed with deepest burgundy and will self-sow. Fantastic with dark-leaved sambucus. Poisonous if eaten.

Hesperis matronalis

Flowers: MAY–JUNE
Height/spread: 90CM X 45CM

This white hesperis is ideal for a twilight border, scenting the air on early summer evenings. It's a hardy biennial that's easy to grow from seed and flowers throughout summer. It readily self-seeds and grows true. Sweet rocket is loved by pollinating insects.

Nicotiana sylvestris (AGM)

Flowers: JULY–OCTOBER
Height/spread: 1.5M X 60CM

The droopy, nodding, tubular trumpets of this white nicotiana let off a gentle vanilla scent at dusk. For best effect, plant in bold drifts in a sunny, sheltered border close to your patio or seating area. Grow in fertile, moist but well-drained soil in full sun or a little shade. The key is to give them space – their lush, exuberant foliage demands elbow room to not look crowded. Good moth plant.

Bulbs

Plant bulbs to add striking highlights and to fill gaps.

Allium 'Mont Blanc'

Flowers: JULY–AUGUST
Height: 1.3M

This showy, reliable allium has baseball-sized globes of starry, shimmering white flowers above strappy, deep-green leaves on tall, slender stems. Plant singly or in small drifts among the foliage of other plants to hide the dying foliage at the base of the stems.

Snowballs of *Allium* 'Mont Blanc' in August.

Tulipa 'Spring Green' .

Allium stipitatum 'Mount Everest'
Flowers: MAY–JUNE
Height/spread: 1.2M
'Mount Everest' flowers before 'Mont Blanc', with large, globular clusters of starry flowers. It has strap-shaped, glossy, grey-green leaves and straight stems, and looks great floating above dark-leaved plants. It's great positioned next to a hedge.

Lilium regale (AGM)
Flowers: JULY
Height/spread: 1.5M
This vigorous white lily is one of the easiest to grow and most sweetly scented. It has white blooms flushed with regal purple on the outside, with a yellow throat and golden anthers. It will tolerate most soils although performs best in humus-rich ground in a sunny spot. Also lovely in containers.

Tulips
Plant tulips in November. Set each bulb point end up in deep 15–18cm holes so their spinnaker-like leaves and flowers don't fall over. If bulbs are to be left in the ground year on year, plant them amongst herbaceous perennials that will mask the tulips, spent foliage as it goes to ground. They like sun and free-draining soil, but if you don't have these conditions tulips will still flower. However, unless they are lifted and stored afterwards (see page 137) their numbers will diminish from year to year.

Tulipa 'Maureen' (AGM)
Flowers: MAY
Height/spread: 60CM
A single, late-flowering tulip bearing snow-white, near-luminous flowers.

Tulipa 'Purissima' (AGM)
Flowers: APRIL
Height/spread: 45CM
Pure white flowers rise majestically above grey-green foliage.

Tulipa 'Rem's Favourite'

Flowers: APRIL–MAY
Height/spread: 45CM
A triumph tulip with pretty flowers bearing purple and ivory-white petals.

Tulipa 'Spring Green' (AGM)
Flowers: MAY
Height/spread: 45CM
A viridiflora tulip with green and ivory-white flowers with light green anthers.

Tulipa 'Swan Wings'
Flowers: APRIL–MAY
Height/spread: 55CM
White, fringed flowers resembling unfurling swan's wings rise above dark green foliage.

Allium buds ready to take over the display once tulips finish flowering.

Tulipa 'White Triumphator' (AGM)
Flowers: MAY
Height/spread: 60CM
A slender and elegant lily-flowered tulip with white, fluted blooms.

Tulipa 'White Dream'
Flowers: APRIL–MAY
Height/spread: 50CM
A triumph tulip bearing single, bowl-shaped white flowers.

Tulipa 'White Marvel'
Flowers: APRIL
Height/spread: 35CM
A single-flowered early tulip, bearing silky white cups above mid-green foliage.

Shrubs and Perennials
These should form the backbone of your scheme.

Artemisia 'Powis Castle' (AGM)
Flowers: AUGUST
Height/spread: 60CM X 90CM
With its billowing filigree-silver leaves, this woody perennial makes a great foil for subtle pastel pinks and whites. The dense silver colour is held through the summer and is at its best in well-drained soil and full sun. It's handy for the edge of borders and makes a good skirt for covering spent tulip foliage.

Anemone 'Honorine Jobert'
Flowers: AUGUST–OCTOBER
Height/spread: 1.2M X 1.5M
See page 114 for details.

Cynara cardunculus (AGM)

Flowers: JUNE–SEPTEMBER
Height/spread: 1.5M X 1.2M

A larger cousin of the globe artichoke, this cardoon is statuesque with silvery-grey leaves and thistle-like purple flowerheads. Cardoons flourish in any well-drained soil, but especially chalky ones, and prefer a position in full sun. They're ideal for a hot, dry, south-facing border, but shelter from strong winds. Protect the crown with a dry mulch in winter.

Eryngium bourgatii 'Picos Amethyst'

Flowers: JULY–AUGUST
Height/spread: 55CM X 50CM

Perennial thistles are ideal for a sunny, well-drained spot, although they like protection from winter wet. This variety has deep blue bracts held on stiff, blue stems and has an almost iridescent glow in moonlight. The foliage is a handsome, dark, marbled green. A great moth plant.

Dahlia 'Joe Swift'

Flowers: JULY–OCTOBER
Height/spread: 90CM X 70CM

Launched at Chelsea in 2009 and named for my great mate, this dahlia was bred using 'Magenta Star' and *Dahlia sorensenii*. It's a beauty, with large white blooms tinged pink as they age and slightly rippled petals like crushed silk. What makes it special is the dark foliage that sets them off. Grow in full sun in moist but well-drained soil.

The purple thistles of cardoons are loved by bees.

Dahlia 'Twyning's After Eight' (AGM)

Flowers: JULY–OCTOBER

Height/spread: 120 X 60CM

This dahlia looks good enough to eat with its chocolate-brown foliage and bright, contrasting white flowers. It's ideal for a twilight border as the white flowers seem to float in thin air at dusk.

Lavandula stoechas (AGM)

Flowers: JUNE–AUGUST

Height/spread: 60CM X 60CM

French lavender has purple drumstick flowers topped with conspicuous, wispy, purple bracts. It grows into compact bushes with grey-green leaves, has a beautiful scent and attracts bees in the daytime. This needs more sun and shelter than most lavenders.

Passiflora caerulea (AGM)

Flowers: JULY–SEPTEMBER

Height/spread: 10M X 1M

This fast-growing climber has rich green leaves and exotic-looking flowers with distinctive purple, white and blue fringed coronas that look a bit like an outlandish tribal costume. The orange-yellow fruits that follow are edible but not tasty. It enjoys a south-facing, sheltered spot with free-draining soil.

Rosa Kew Gardens (Ausfence)

Flowers: JUNE–OCTOBER

Height/spread: 1.5M X 1M

This thornless rose is a breakthrough in rose breeding, bred to mark Kew Garden's 250th anniversary. It's rude with health and produces lots of small, vanilla-white single flowers tinged with lemon. It repeat flowers and produces clusters of marble-sized red hips. Grow in a sunny, well-drained site in fertile soil.

Sambucus nigra f. porphyrophylla 'Eva'

Flowers: JUNE

Height/spread: 3M X 2M

A magnificent black, lacy-leaved elderberry that resembles a Japanese maple, but is easier to care for. Plants are emblazoned by massive umbels of pink flowers in summer, which release a lemony fragrance into the air. Grow in humus-rich, well-drained soil.

'"Joe Swift" is a beauty, with large white blooms tinged pink as they age and slightly rippled petals like crushed silk'

Snapdragon buds push up through cow parsley lookalike, *Ammi majus*.

The spinnaker-like foliage of tulips pushing up in early spring.

Your maintenance regime

A floriferous scheme like this needs regular tending to keep it in tip-top shape. Follow these pointers and you'll be on the right track.

Spring
- Coppice established sambucus in early spring to a 50cm stump to encourage large, fresh leaves and apply a balanced fertiliser and a mulch of garden compost.
- Tidy the tatty leaves of astelia and cynara by cutting them back to their bases.
- Trim lavender and artemisia to the buds emerging from woody stems, avoiding old wood.
- Look out for aphids on emerging tulip foliage. Spray off with a mineral soap.
- Pot up dahlia tubers and grow on in a light, frost-free place.
- Sow annuals according to their packet instructions.
- Divide or take basal cuttings from lychnis.
- Deadhead tulips after flowering, but let leaves die back to return nutrients to the bulb.
- Lift tulip bulbs once foliage has died down and store in boxes somewhere cool and dry for replanting in autumn.
- Trim dead growth from passion flowers after the last spring frost.
- Check for suckers on roses and pull them from the plant if you find them.
- Sow biennial foxgloves under glass in seed compost at 18–29°C.

Summer
- Trowel up self-sown lychnis and foxgloves and replant where they are to flower.
- Watch out for red lily beetles, pick off and squash if seen.
- Remove any self-sown plants that have reverted and lost their white colour.
- Deadhead perennials and roses.
- Take cuttings of lavender and artemisia for plants for free (see page 73).
- Shear over lavender and artemisia when flowers finish, cutting 5cm into foliage to stop it becoming leggy.
- On hungry soils, feed roses with chicken pellets to give them a boost.
- Sow biennial hesperis in late spring/early summer at 15–18°C. Plant out in early autumn.

Autumn
- Plant spring-flowering bulbs (leave tulips until November).
- Cut down frost-blackened dahlia stems, cover them with a sheet of plastic and top with 12cm of compost. Alternatively lift tubers in late autumn and overwinter in a frost-free place.

Winter
- Apply a balanced fertiliser and mulch in late winter or early spring.
- Cut untidy spent perennials down to their crown.
- Prune roses. On young plants, remove any wayward stems and those that cross at the centre. On established plants cut out some of the older wood to encourage healthy new growth from the base.
- Take root cuttings from eryngiums.

Techniques for the Twilight Garden

The main aim in developing a twilight garden is to maintain and enhance the colour scheme, removing any self-sown colour rogues and keeping the succession going. Keep edges filled with silver plants to hide the green legs of taller white-flowered plants and consider adding hard landscaping with pergolas, arbours and arches and grow roses Sissinghurst-style over them to add white shades at eye level and above. Lift any sombre-looking paving by encouraging white flowers, such as erigeron, to colonise the cracks and soften walls and fences by clothing them in colour.

Planting into the side of a wall

A raised pond made from stacked slate forms a focal point to the Twilight Garden. The gaps between the slates, like dry stone walls and rock gardens, are particularly good for succulents and alpine plants. I planted up the sides with self-sowing white alyssum and purple-leaved house leeks (*Sempervivum*) to create a colour link between the pond and the borders. To 'glue' plants in place while waiting for roots to grow and anchor them, make a sticky mix of garden soil and some well-rotted manure and press it into the gaps to receive the plants (1). Bought pots of house leeks look most natural if you split the roots into smaller portions before planting, and they go further (2 and 3).

1

2

3

Taking root cuttings

Sea hollies look spectacular when grown in groups but you need lots of plants. Propagating from root cuttings is the cheapest solution. Do this any time from autumn to spring.

Scrape soil from the base of the plant to reveal its roots (1), and use secateurs to cut 10cm lengths of pencil-thick roots from the side of the plant (2). Pot up three at a time into a 12cm container filled with moist multi-purpose compost with the thicker end (the top) just showing above the compost (3). Cover the roots of the parent plant and water well. Keep the cuttings in a frost-free greenhouse or cold frame and they will sprout from the top within 3–6 weeks.

You can propogate Crambe, dicentra, Echinacea and autumn-flowering anemone in this way.

1

2

3

How to trap and identify moths

Take a wander around your garden on a still summer evening and you'll be amazed at the life there. Moths are an essential part of the food chain, sustaining many birds, bats and other mammals in our gardens. In fact, Butterfly Conservation estimate that blue-tit chicks alone devour 35 billion caterpillars every year in Britain, so any drop is bad news for birds.

As moths are attracted to light sources, one of the most basic and cheap ways of seeing them up close is to spread out a large white sheet and suspend a light above it or in front of it (below). The type of light source is important. Whilst an ordinary light bulb can attract a few species, specialist bulbs, such as a grow light or a mercury vapour bulb (which costs around £12 from a DIY shop), are much more effective. Remember different moths fly at different times of night and at different times of the year.

To identify moths, you need to look at them closely. To do this, put a finger in front of the moth's nose and, nine times out of 10, it'll hop on. Don't try to pick up moths as this can harm them and, in some cases, can cause skin irritation.

This is an entertaining way to spend a summer evening, and something educational to do with children, who love the drama and suspense of the hunt. For more information on identifying moths, check out www.mothscount.org which runs an annual recording scheme that the public can get involved in.

Know your moths

Hundreds of different moths visit our gardens, and even a small urban plot can support more than 100 species. You just need a good mix of plants including shrubs and trees as well as longer grass and flowers. Grow native hedges, such as hawthorn, as food plants for larvae.

We have around 2,400 species of moth in the UK; 800 of which are large like butterflies (the rest are small micro-moths) and most cause little or no damage to garden plants. Some people find them quite frightening as they masquerade as being fiercer than they are, with faux eyes on their thorax, Biggles-like spectacles and hairy bodies. These markings are only there to scare predators, though. The large moths are divided into 19 families, all closely related to each other. Each family shares certain characteristics, some of which can be recognised by a beginner. In particular, members of a family tend to be a similar shape, so this is a good thing to take note of first.

NOCTUIDS is the largest family, with just more than 400 members. They are nearly all active at night, have powerful, agile flight and often need to refuel with nectar. Noctuids have thick bodies and a characteristic resting posture; the wings are held overlapping across the back, making a tent-like shape. Viewed from above the moth looks like a narrow triangle or letter A. Noctuids tend to be subtly coloured, often a mixture of browns and greys.

GEOMETRIDS is the next-largest family, with more than 300 species. They have thin bodies and most hold their wings flat in a butterfly shape when resting. They have rather weak fluttering flight and, as many fly at dusk, dawn and in the daytime, they are often mistaken for butterflies. The geometrids include several large sub-families, notably the waves, carpets and pugs. The family name comes from the Greek for ground-measurer, after the odd looping walk of their caterpillars.

TIGERS AND ERMINES are in the family called Arctiidae. Most tiger moths have dark forewings spotted or striped with white or cream, while their hind wings and bodies are a vivid red, orange or yellow. These bright colours warn predators that they taste unpleasant. Also in this family are the small slender footman moths, which are shaped rather like pumpkin seeds when resting. The White Ermine and Buff Ermine, as their name suggests, resemble fur.

HAWK MOTHS are big and include Britain's largest resident moth, the Privet Hawk-moth. They have fat bodies and narrow, swept-back wings for fast, powerful flight. The Bee Hawk-moths may not be recognised as moths at all, as they look just like bumble bees, with fat furry bodies and transparent wings. This helps them avoid being eaten by predators, which assume they can sting (they can't). Another family called the Clearwings use the same trick, pretending to be wasps. Humming-bird hawk-moths fly by day and hover in front of flowers such as lavender to suck out nectar with their long tongues.

Catmint is a valuable source of nectar.

2 | THE BEE BORDER

Of our 25 native Bumblebee species, three have become extinct in the last 50 years, and the UK Biodiversity Action Plan has identified a further seven native bees as under threat. It's an alarming trend, not least because a third of our diet is directly dependent on bees pollinating crops. Many fruits, vegetables and nuts simply would not exist without their help.

No single factor is to blame for the collapse, although pesticide use and loss of hedgerows and habitat due to farming has played a large part. A decrease in wildflowers, marshes, hay meadows and flower-filled grassland has also had an impact.

Don't panic. You can do something to help by planting flowers for bees to feed from, and places for them to nest and reproduce. It doesn't have to be a wild-flower meadow either, many perennial plants are filled with nectar and pollen that bees love.

The Bee Border at Greenacre is 3 metres deep and 10 metres wide, and runs alongside a path connecting the Seed Packet Meadows and the Twilight Garden. It's surrounded by a low hedge of Lavandula x chaytoriae 'Sawyers' (AGM) and dissected by a beech hedge which acts as a wind break and another holing-up habitat for bees. As the border of which I'm most proud, it is colourful for a huge chunk of the year, and includes a diverse range of plants while still offering coherence and winter structure. When I look at it in full bloom, I always think of what Greenacre looked like before we started gardening here. It's amazing that just two short years ago this place was pretty much a wildlife-free zone and now it literally buzzes with life.

In a nutshell: *this border is a collection of nectar- and pollen-rich plants that bees love. It comprises herbaceous perennials, a lavender hedge for winter structure and lots of bee boxes*

Suited to: *create this scheme if you want to attract wildlife and love a purply-blue colour scheme and scent*

Ideal location: *a sheltered, sunny spot is essential*

Space needed: *you need a minimum of two square metres*

Maintenance rating: *moderate. You'll need to look after a border like this throughout the year, although no tricky skills are required*

Eco credentials: *excellent. These plants are popular with bees, hoverflies, lacewings and butterflies. They also produce seedheads for sparrows and finches to feed on*

Bee boxes

Verbena bonariensis
running throughout.

1: *Erysimum* 'Bowles's Mauve'
2: *Geranium* Rozanne
3: Drumstick alliums in early
    summer
4: *Trifolium rubens*
5: *Knautia macedonica*
6: *Verbena rigida*
7: *Echium candicans*
8: *Helenium autumnale*
9: *Nepeta* 'Six Hills Giant'
10: *Angelica archangelica*
11: *Cirsium rivulare*
    'Atropurpureum'
12: *Polemonium caeruleum*
13: *Daphne bholua*
    'Jacqueline Postill'
14: *Pulmonaria* 'Blue Ensign'
15: *Echium vulgare*
16: *Veronicastrum virginicum*
    'Erica'
17: *Salvia nemorosa*
    'Caradonna'
18: *Echinops bannaticus*
    'Taplow Blue'
19: *Monarda* 'Fishes'
20: *Aster lateriflorus*
    'Lady in Black'
21: *Tanacetum coccineum*
    Robinson's red-flowered
22: *Sedum spectabile*
23: Lavender 'Sawyers'
    hedge underplanted
    with *Allium
    sphaerocephalon*

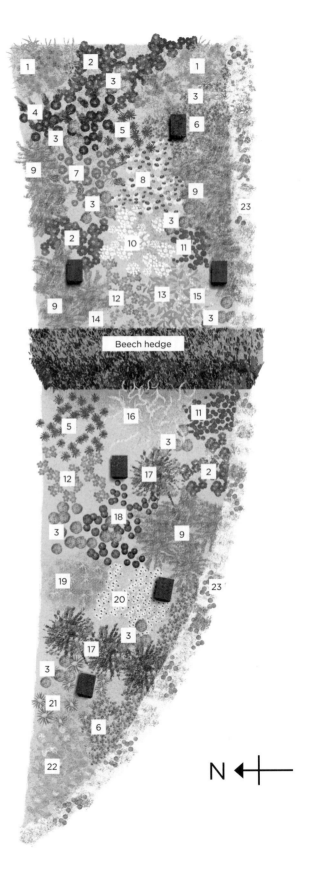

Beech hedge

N

Bee Border elements

Flowers

Bees prefer flowers that are close to the ground with simple, single blooms. Aim to have something in flower virtually every month of the growing season, as the first bees emerge from hibernation as early as February.

Diversity

Avoid huge swathes of the same flower, aiming for a range of flower shapes and sizes to favour both short- and long-tongued bees.

Shelter

Create your border in a sunny, sheltered spot. It will be visited by bees more than a shady or exposed site.

Habitat

Hollow-stemmed plants and hibernation boxes filled with short lengths of bamboo, provide a sheltered and warm environment for bees and hoverflies in winter. A dry pile of leaves underneath a hedge also does the trick.

Know your bees

Bumblebees are the best known, with their furry striped bodies and bumbling flight. They're less aggressive than honey bees and will create small colonies of up to a few hundred, with a queen and worker bees. At the end of the season the worker bees die, while the mated queen overwinters to set up a new colony the following year. It's these big bumblebees that you see on warm days early in the year, having just emerged from hibernation and in search of flowers for a meal.

Honey bees are farmed for their honey in hives and live in huge colonies. They are also striped, but smaller, and only furry on their heads and thorax, and are often mistaken for wasps. By the time you see a honey bee in your garden it would have been promoted through a hierarchy of jobs: cleaning the nest, feeding the larvae, removing water from nectar to turn it into honey, processing pollen, guarding the nest and then taking orientation flights. After three to six weeks they're out in your garden gathering nectar, pollen and water for the hive.

Solitary bees are the largest group in the UK, including many that frequent our gardens such as the mason, carpenter and leafcutter types. Solitary bees are small and can look like furry versions of honey bees and wasps. Rather than living in groups, males set up territories around flowers while the female makes a nest alone. Mining bees do this in the ground, while leafcutter and carpenter bees choose soft, pithy wood, fence posts, cracks and crevices. Mason bees, as their name suggests, search for easy-to-tunnel joints in old lime-mortar walls.

My plant choices

A succession of flowers from early spring right through until late autumn is the key to a successful bee border, and it's vital you have something to offer the first female bumblebee queens that have survived winter hibernation. They often wake as early as February, hungry for food and eager to start new colonies. Like the workers that emerge later in the season, they gather two things from flowers: sugary liquid nectar and pollen. Bees lap up nectar like an energy drink from the base of the blooms, while scooping pollen into sacks on their legs to use for honey and feeding their young.

Like meals on a menu, some flowers appeal more than others, and those with high levels of protein in their pollen are firm favourites (those in the mint family, *Lamiaceae* – salvia and catmint – are good). Quantity is also important and plants like wallflowers, which produce close clusters of flowers, save bees expending energy between food stops. As a general rule, simple single flowers are most appealing to bees as double blooms (with petals arranged in complicated designs) often come at the expense of nectar or pollen and are difficult for the bees to access.

All of these plants here are perfect for attracting and supporting a bee population. Use them in your garden to help turn around bee decline.

Alliums

Because every allium flower head is a mass of blooms, they make great fast food for bees. All they need is full sun and a well-drained soil. We've planted four different varieties through the border to give a succession of stand-out colour.

A. hollandicum 'Purple Sensation' (AGM)
Flowers: MAY–JUNE
Height/spread: 90CM X 20CM
Neat lavender-purple flowers make this a Chelsea flower show favourite.

A. schubertii
Flowers: JUNE
Height/spread: 40CM X 20CM
Looser and later heads than 'Globemaster', resembling a firework in mid-burst.

A. 'Globemaster' (AGM)

Flowers: JUNE
Height/spread: 90CM X 20CM
'Globemaster' can produce a thousand flowers or more on just one head.

'It's vital you have something to offer the first female bumblebee queens that have survived winter hibernation. They often wake as early as February, hungry for food and eager to start new colonies.'

A. cristophii (AGM)

Flowers: JUNE–JULY
Height/spread: 60CM X 15CM
For giant 20cm heads, try this AGM winner.

A. sphaerocephalon

Flowers: JULY–AUGUST
Height/spread: 60CM X 5CM

Small pink to reddish-brown, egg-shaped drumsticks on tall wiry stems. The flowers are densely packed and bloom for many weeks. Plant to grow through lavender.

Angelica archangelica

Flowers: MAY–JULY
Height/spread: 2M X 1.5M
Angelica is loved by bees and hoverflies and is just the thing for introducing a bit of structure. It flowers in summer and looks like cow parsley on acid, with 2.5m stems covered in lime-cordial-coloured umbels. This spectacular show takes its toll and the plant promptly dies. The seed is perfectly viable, though, and should be sown as soon as it's plump and ripe, straight in the soil where you want new plants to grow, or in

pots left out in the cold over winter. Treat angelica as a biennial and grow it in sun, keeping the roots moist.

Cirsium rivulare 'Atropurpureum'

Flowers: JULY–AUGUST
Height/spread: 1.2M X 90CM

This ornamental thistle provides crimson landing pads for bees and enjoys sun or light shade. If you keep removing the spent flower spikes, it'll continue flowering into early autumn. Cirsium likes rich conditions, so add plenty of compost or well-rotted manure to your planting hole. Cut back the leaves for a fresh flush when they start to look tatty in late summer. Divide by splitting rosettes when they start to look congested.

Daphne bholua 'Jacqueline Postill' (AGM)

Flowers: JANUARY–FEBRUARY
Height/spread: 2M X 1.5M

Just-awake bees need nectar to feed on in late winter and early spring, and this daphne is a lovely flower to greet them. It has a delicate lemon scent and pink/white star-shaped blooms. This slow-growing shrub likes a sunny, sheltered place where its scent can linger. It's also happy in a container.

Echinops bannaticus 'Taplow Blue'

Flowers: JUNE–AUGUST
Height/spread: 1.2M X 75CM

A fantastic plant for wildlife gardens, attracting bees and butterflies like a magnet. Its flowers, which are prickly, blue, 8cm baubles, look like a cross between an allium and a thistle. This is a broad-shouldered plant and will quickly grow to a metre wide. Clumps often become crowded and die out in the middle, so lift and divide in spring every few years to rejuvenate. Echinops also spread from self-sown seed. Perennial sunflowers (*Helianthus*) make a good plant partner for filling large borders fast.

Hide the posts of bee boxes with sprawlers like catmint.

The bee boxes add a whimsical look to borders and valuable homes for overwintering bumblebees.

Echium candicans (AGM)

Flowers: JUNE
Height/spread: 1.8M X 1.2M

A shrubby echium, making domes of metallic blue leaves topped with candle-like 30cm-tall flower spikes. It's most suited to mild parts of the country (cities and the South West, etc.) where full sun and shelter in winter is guaranteed. I grow this from seed and plant out every summer, keeping my fingers crossed for a clement winter.

Echium vulgare (viper's bugloss)

Flowers: JUNE–SEPTEMBER
Height/spread: 50CM X 40CM

This is a native biennial for growing in gravel, borders or amongst the long grass in a meadow. It thrives on alkaline, chalky or sandy soils in sun. Leave the seed to fall to create self-perpetuating colonies.

Erysimum 'Bowles's Mauve' (AGM)

Flowers: FEBRUARY–JULY and beyond
Height/spread: 75CM X 60CM

A perennial wallflower with unrivalled stamina, which forms wide boulders or blue-grey leaves smothered with spikes of mauve blooms. All this flowering takes its toll and plants will need replacing after a couple of seasons. Take cuttings in summer (see page 73) and overwinter them in case plants get killed off by winter wet and cold.

'Domes of metallic blue leaves topped with candle-like flower spikes'

Geranium Rozanne (AGM)

Flowers: JUNE–SEPTEMBER
Height/spread: 75CM X 1M

An unfussy cranesbill (aka 'Gerwat'), this has large saucer-shaped blooms and flowers for a long time in both sunny and shady spots.

Knautia macedonica

Flowers: JULY–SEPTEMBER
Height/spread: 80CM X 80CM
With low-lying, jagged leaves and dozens of wiry stems topped with crimson pin cushions, this scabious lookalike is happiest in full sun. It flowers endlessly in summer but can succumb to mildew on very poor soils, in hot summers, or if it's crowded out by neighbouring plants. Give it room to peek through other plants – it's gorgeous with stipa and medium-sized grasses – and cut back any affected foliage to encourage fresh, new growth. It's not only bees that benefit from this plant – hoverflies like it and the ripening seedheads are attractive to birds.

Lavandula x chaytoriae 'Sawyers' (AGM)

Flowers: JULY–AUGUST
Height/spread: 50CM X 50CM
This lavender has dark purple flowers and is renowned for its lovely silver foliage. It stays compact and in good shape over winter, and given good drainage (improve with grit if yours is poor) and a sunny spot it'll take temperatures down to -15°C. Do not improve the fertility of the soil in any way. Fertiliser and/or organic matter are to be avoided at all costs as they lead to soft, sappy growth and an open, gaping plant.

Monarda 'Fishes'
Flowers: JULY–AUGUST
Height/spread: 1.2M X 60CM
Pale pink, shrimp-like petals flower for a long time. Keep moist to avoid powdery mildew in summer.

Nepeta 'Six Hills Giant'
Flowers: JUNE–JULY
Height/spread: 60CM X 90CM
This catmint's sprawling habit makes it the perfect plant for edging a path and planting underneath taller, leggy plants like shrub roses. Chop it back to the crown after flowering for a fresh flush of foliage and the chance of more lilac blooms. Trouble-free and easy, it's fine in full sun or part-shade in ordinary soil. If cats threaten to love it to death, put a few peasticks amongst the leaves to keep them at bay.

Polemonium caeruleum
Flowers: JUNE
Height/spread: 80CM X 30CM
A dainty perennial with purple-blue, bell-like flowers. Fine in both sun or part-shade. This plant needs moisture around its roots and loves lashings of compost at planting time. Collected seed is easy to germinate if sown in the autumn or spring and kept in a cold frame to sprout.

Pulmonaria 'Blue Ensign'
Flowers: MARCH–MAY
Height/spread: 30CM X 30CM
One for the early bees, this lungwort is one of the best blues for spring and has bristly, untypically neat and narrow, dark green leaves spotted with white. It will tolerate sun

The *Lamiaceae* family of plants are firm favourites with bees.

but it's happiest in shady, moist woodland-type situations. It often succumbs to mildew as summer comes on, but if you shear back the foliage to the crown, feed and water it fresh new growth will shortly follow.

Salvia nemorosa 'Caradonna'

Flowers: JUNE–OCTOBER
Height/spread: 75CM X 45CM
Hardy salvias are a magnet for bees, butterflies and moths in summer and, deadheaded, this compact version flowers non-stop for months. Give it a sunny well-drained spot and its strikingly dark, violet flowers and stems can't fail to impress.

Tanacetum coccineum
Robinson's red-flowered
Flowers: MAY–JULY
Height/spread: 70CM X 45CM
This plant flowers for weeks if the blooms are regularly removed as they go over. Its fern-like foliage has a tangy aroma (like its common herb-garden cousin tansy, or *Tanacetum vulgare*) and it has showy crimson flowers akin to a chrysanthemum. It doesn't spread as freely as tansy, so the way to bulk up numbers and keep the colour is by taking basal cuttings during the spring (see page 153). This is also a good plant for a cutting garden, although it needs staking to look its best.

Trifolium rubens
Flowers: JULY–AUGUST
Height/spread: 60CM X 60CM
Unlike the clover in your lawn, this species is

a bushy, upright perennial with blue-green foliage and large, deep red flowers. It makes a lovely cut flower and can also be sown as a green manure. Bees can't get enough of it.

Verbena rigida

Flowers: JUNE–SEPTEMBER
Height/spread: 50CM X 40CM

For long-flowering purple spikes through summer you can't beat this plant. It's related to *Verbena bonariensis*, although is much shorter and perfect for the front of a border and along pathways. It used to be considered as borderline hardy, but given good drainage and a mild area tubers can overwinter in the ground. In colder, wetter areas, lift tubers and store under cover as you would a dahlia.

Veronicastrum virginicum 'Erica'

Flowers: JULY–AUGUST
Height/spread: 1.5M X 50CM

Dark stems and pink flower spikes make this a statuesque plant for a bee border. This cultivar is smaller than most and does best in rich, moist soil in full sun or light shade. Staking isn't necessary with veronicastrums, and slugs don't usually go for them, which is a bonus!

'Hardy salvias are a magnet for bees, butterflies and moths in summer'

Plants with numerous flowers mean bees spend less energy searching for food.

Your maintenance regime

You need to keep on top of a bee border throughout the year, although if you follow these simple steps you can't go far wrong.

Spring
- Put out wildlife-friendly slug pellets or traps.
- Trim lavender into neat 20cm hummocks just as it starts to grow, but avoid cutting into woody old growth.
- Stake perennials that will eventually grow tall with peasticks.
- Mulch with 5cm of garden compost to conserve moisture and keep down weeds. This is essential around *Cirsium rivulare* and monarda to prevent powdery mildew.

Summer
- Trim lavender after it finishes flowering to encourage a flush of bushy growth.
- Deadhead flowers, such as tanacetum, to lengthen their display.
- Cut back nepeta after flowering for a fresh flush of foliage in September.
- Take cuttings of lavender and perennial wallflowers (see opposite).

Autumn
- Collect seed.
- Lift *Verbena ridiga* if you live in a cold and wet area.
- Cover echiums to overwinter and protect from frost.
- Pot up seedlings of self-sown plants and replant where they are to flower, or pot on for planting out next spring.

Winter
- Clear away and compost spent stems. Leave them on the top of the heap for a few days in case any larvae haven't hatched and taken flight.
- Collect cut hollow stems to refresh bee boxes next year and keep in a dry shed over winter.

Bees gathering from spires of *Veronicastrum virginicum* 'Erica'.

Techniques for the Bee Border

For the Bee Border it's all about growing as many nectar-rich plants as cheaply as you can to attract bees and other beneficial insects. After that you just have to make sure you keep them.

Grow a lavender hedge from cuttings

Save on the cost of lavenders by growing a hedge from cuttings. Lavenders put on a flush of bushy growth that roots really well a few weeks after the spent flowers have been sheared away in summer. Snip half a dozen 8–12cm lengths of flower-free stem (1), trim just below the lowest leaf and pinch off all the leaves from the lower half of each cutting (2). Push cuttings around the rim of a 9cm pot filled with multi-purpose compost blended with a handful of horticultural grit (3). Top the compost with grit and place in a shallow tray of water to soak (4). After 8 weeks in a cold frame, watered every fortnight, they'll have rooted and be ready for potting on individually. Keep pots on the dry side over winter in a cold frame or greenhouse, and plant out 45cm apart in spring. This technique works for perennial wallflowers too.

How to make a bee box

Feeding bees is relatively easy, but providing a habitat for overwintering bumble bees and solitary bees takes a bit of creativity. I make my own bee boxes from bamboo and hollow stems, held aloft on poles. They're a bit like bird boxes, but instead of a solid front with a hole for a bird, they have lots of smaller holes.

I painted the bee boxes at Greenacre in bright colours to give the bee border a colourful skyline (use a solvent-free, eco-friendly paint). The boxes offer digs for bees and provide a winter home for other beneficial insects like aphid-eating lacewings and hoverflies. Along with helping bees, the boxes look pretty, add height and also bring a sense of magic and whimsy to the border. You will know bees have taken residence when the ends of the cane are sealed with pieces of leaf. Refresh the stems in summer once the old canes have disintegrated.

You will need:
A 1.2m length of 12 x 1.5cm timber | A slate tile and small strip of lead for the roof | Workbench Wood saw | Hollow sticks or cut pieces of bamboo cane | Pencil | Ruler | Wood screws | Solvent-free, eco-friendly paint | Gloves | Pliers | Flat-headed galvanised tacks | Drill | Hammer | 1.5m tall post

---

1: Create the sides, back and base of the box from the length of timber. The sides should be 20cm tall. The base should be 12 x 13.5cm and the back should be approximately 30cm tall.

2: Make the sides by securing two lengths of the timber together in the jaws of a work bench. Mark a 45-degree line across the sides of the timber and down the face on each side in pencil. Carefully cut along the line with a wood saw. Cut another piece of timber for the back and use the angled sides as a guide to give the angle of the roof, then cut the angled sides. Again, if the two are laid one on top of the other and clamped in place while cutting they will, when one is flipped over, end up the mirror image of each other.

3: Drill pilot holes in the back and fix the sides to it with woodscrews, then attach the base in the same way.

4: Paint the whole structure with solvent-free, eco-friendly paint.

5: Make the top from roofing slate sawn in half with an old wood saw. Drill holes in the slate and wood so that only gentle hammering is necessary and fix it in place with flat-headed galvanised tacks. Always wear work gloves as the edges can be sharp.

6: Bend a short piece of lead and place it over the ridge of the roof to create a neat join between the slates. It will hold itself in place.

7: Fix the box to a 1.5m timber post driven into the soil. Use a couple of screws through the base of the box to secure it. Fill the box with hollow stems collected from the garden or short lengths of bamboo cane. Orientate the box towards the morning sunshine so that it's warmed quickly in winter.

Fragrant lilies and aniseed-scented fennel line the cobble path of the Scented Front Garden.

3 | THE SCENTED FRONT GARDEN

Your front garden is always on show, with passers-by and neighbours all having the chance to take a peek and tell you what they make of your creation. So why not offer them something a little extra? When creating front gardens both for myself and other people, I always make scented plants a priority. They'll give you, and your neighbours, no end of daily pleasure, and on warm days they will waft their wonderful fragrance down an entire street.

The front garden I created at Greenacre is my idea of scented loveliness. It's a roughly triangular plot, 5 metres each side, with the long diagonal side closest to the 'street'. It is divided into three beds dissected by cobble paths and a central cobble roundel (see project on page 90) providing the routes to the side gate and front door. The garden is entered via an iron arch set in railings, which I've planted with roses to make the garden look welcoming. The house façade faces both south and east, effectively trapping the heat of the sun and the perfume of the plants. Anywhere enclosed, where air tends to warm up during the day, is ideal for making the most of scented plants.

The planting is tightly packed to give a feeling of privacy without resorting to oppressive hedging and fences. The mix of perennials changes through the growing season to give a succession of flowers, and helps to soften the hard landscaping and front of the house. To restrain the hustle and bustle of the numerous plants, I've limited the colour scheme to silver, lemon, purple and green, providing a cohesive look and an appearance neat enough to keep up with the Joneses, or, in my case, the Swifts and the Fowlers!

In a nutshell: *this scheme is a mix of fragrant, cottage-inspired perennials and shrubs that are specially chosen for front garden situations*

Suited to: *this style is for you if you like a romantic yet structured look*

Ideal location: *a small suntrap with average soil is all you need, although this scheme would also work in semi-shade*

Space needed: *you need a minimum of 4 square metres*

Maintenance rating: *moderate. It'll need one blitz per season, along with regular weeding, pruning and staking*

Eco credentials: *excellent. This is an eco-friendly alternative to a paved front garden and many of the plants are attractive to bees and beneficial insects*

Scented Front Garden elements

Plants

Keep your plant scheme as informal as possible, but remember that cottage-style flowery schemes can look untidy if you don't keep on top of maintenance (see pages 86–87).

Pathway

The priority with a front garden is to get to the front door, so plan the paths first and the borders second. Functionality is key, and paths must be wide enough for your wheelie bin and any other gubbins you may have (recycling boxes, bikes, etc.). Buy cobbles or slabs from stone merchants and online.

Paintwork colour

Greys and blue-greens complement flowers without outshining their colours.

Cobble roundel

When two or more paths meet, the join will often look awkward. A roundel is a simple design feature that ties paths together neatly, opens up the centre of a garden and offers a place for guests to muster outside the front door.

Vine eyes and wires

These are a small-garden essential and are a great way of packing out a garden without it feeling overcrowded. Fixed in horizontal rows every 60cm up a wall, taut wires provide a framework for tying back shrubs and climbers.

Ironwork railings

Reclaimed from a salvage yard, our see-through ironwork railings provide a neat boundary that allows plants to get the light they need to thrive. Round-topped railings are ideal as they as you won't catch your clothes on them as you pass by.

Archway

A simple ironwork arch accentuates the entrance and allows flowers to grow, be enjoyed and sniffed at head height.

Windowboxes and containers

A window ledge is a great opportunity for a plant-filled box, and containers of scented lilies in summer enhance fragrance and colour (see page 89). Fix or padlock pots or weigh down with pebbles if security is an issue.

Waterbutt

If you can squeeze in a waterbutt, and have an available downpipe, do it. It'll provide easy access to water without having to trail a mucky hosepipe through your house. You can buy attractive oak barrels, although economical, plastic butts can be hidden behind a hazel screen and climbing plants.

Screens

Use natural materials such as hazel to create screens while you're waiting for plants to mature to hide waterbutts, recycling boxes and wheelie bins.

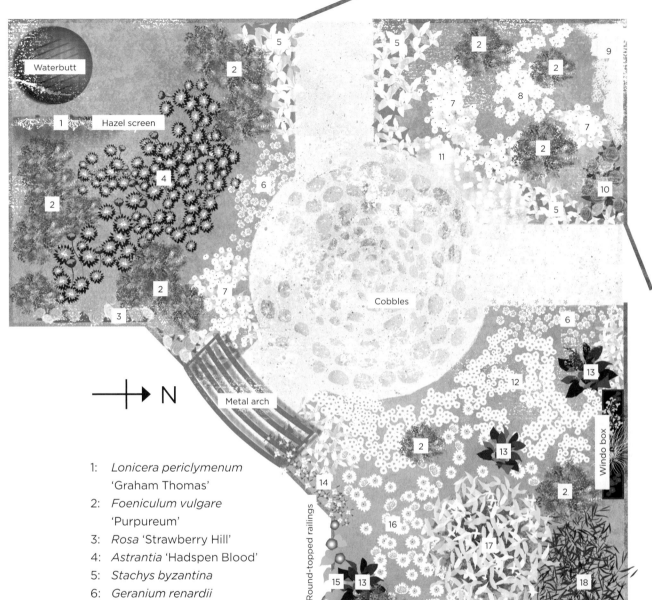

Waterbutt

1 Hazel screen

Cobbles

Metal arch

N

Round-topped railings

Windo box

Willow screen

1: *Lonicera periclymenum*
   'Graham Thomas'
2: *Foeniculum vulgare*
   'Purpureum'
3: *Rosa* 'Strawberry Hill'
4: *Astrantia* 'Hadspen Blood'
5: *Stachys byzantina*
6: *Geranium renardii*
7: *Lychnis coronaria* 'Alba'
8: *Phlox paniculata*
   'Mount Fuji'
9: *Cytisus battandieri*
10: *Rosa* Gertrude Jekyll
11: *Dianthus* 'Miss Sinkins'
12: *Anthemis tinctoria*
13: *Atriplex hortensis*
    var. *rubra*
14: *Clematis* x *triternata*
    'Rubromarginata'

15: Morning Glory on railings
16: *Astrantia major* subsp.
    involucrata 'Shaggy'
17: *Elaeagnus* 'Quicksilver'
    (trained in a lollipop)
18: *Sambucus nigra* f.
    porphyrophylla 'Eva'

79

My plant choices

For a scented cottage scheme, choose plants which bloom for a long period, like astrantia and repeat-flowering roses. This will allow you to stick to a small palette, which looks simple and less fussy than a dolly mixture of varieties. Repeat colours using different plants, for example bronze-purple smoke bush with bronze fennel, and embellish with bulbs. Don't just think about flowers, though – foliage can also provide colours and textures, tying a whole garden together.

Burglar-deterrent or not, I don't like overly prickly plants (other than roses that can be trained out of the way) in front gardens as they trap every stray piece of litter, and can snag as you pass by. The same goes for anything poisonous, such as euphorbia which releases skin-irritant sap if the stems are bruised or broken. Save these plants for the back garden where there's less passing traffic.

Herbaceous Perennials
For non-stop flower and scent.

Anthemis tinctoria
Flowers: MAY–JULY
Height/spread: 60CM X 60CM
A jolly perennial with white, yellow-centred daisies on tweedy silver stems. Trim back spent stems to the ground after flowering to encourage a fresh flush of foliage, and maybe even flowers. This plant makes a floppy skirt, ideal for hiding the bare legs of roses.

Astrantia 'Hadspen Blood'

Flowers: JUNE–AUGUST
Height/spread: 60CM X 45CM
This Ribena-red perennial has winged, pincushion flowers. It will grow in full sun but produces the best colour in part-shade. The flowers look good as they fade, although cut it back if it looks tatty and you might be rewarded with a flush of fresh growth. Keep plants moist by adding lots of compost at planting time and by mulching in autumn. This astrantia produces seed that comes true, which is an added bonus.

Astrantia major
subsp. *involucrata* 'Shaggy' (AGM)

Anthemis tinctoria
makes a great
peek-a-boo plant
for railings.

Flowers: JUNE–AUGUST
Height/spread: 80CM X 45CM
This is similar to 'Hadspen Blood', only it's taller and the flowers are white with a green tinge to the ruff. It's a superb filler for around taller, more structural plants, with its long-lasting, easy-to-grow blooms. Grow in the same way as 'Hadspen Blood'.

Dianthus 'Miss Sinkins'
Flowers: JULY–SEPTEMBER
Height/spread: 30CM X 30CM
A cottage-garden classic with white-fringed petals and a vanilla scent. It can become leggy and start to die out after time, so create new plants from tip cuttings in summer.

Foeniculum vulgare 'Purpureum'
Flowers: AUGUST
Height/spread: 1.8M X 60CM
Bronze fennel is a tall, vase-shaped perennial herb with an aniseed scent and auburn tassels of foliage. I planted it in all three borders of my Greenacre front garden, to tie the whole space together. Its primary purpose is as a backdrop so, although its yellow umbels are attractive enough, I prefer to chop plants down before they flower to encourage fresh fronds. I do let some flower as they self-seed readily, making it easy to propagate new plants.

Geranium renardii (AGM)
Flowers: JUNE–JULY
Height/spread: 30CM X 30CM
A handsome perennial with a neat quality that's ideal for edging paths and softening hard landscape. It stays low to the ground and the white, purple-veined flowers do well in full sun or a little shade. This is an easy and undemanding plant – just cut it back to the ground in autumn when the foliage starts to look tired.

Lychnis coronaria 'Alba' (AGM)
Flowers: JULY–AUGUST
Height/spread: 80CM X 45CM
A silver, felt-leaved plant with white, saucer-shaped flowers with a pink kiss in the centre. This classic cottage-garden perennial is short-lived (two or three years) and it tends to succumb to rot in wet summers. That said, it self-seeds around and pops up to fill any gaps, although it does tend to revert to the clashing bright-pink species. It's best in sunny, dry spots that are typical of so many front gardens and works well at the front of a border between other plants.

Phlox paniculata 'Mount Fuji' (AGM)

Flowers: AUGUST–OCTOBER
Height/spread: 90CM X 90CM

This pretty phlox has white flowers that fill the garden with a delicate scent through late summer and autumn. It thrives in sun or part-shade, and does well in soil that stays moist during the summer. Achieve this by adding plenty of compost when planting and mulch with more in spring. Stake with peasticks in spring to prevent the large clusters of blooms from flopping. Take root cuttings (see page 57), or divide established clumps in winter, to create new plants for free.

Stachys byzantina
Flowers: not grown for flowers
Height/spread: 45CM X 60CM
Also know as lamb's ears, this plant is a great silver-leaved edger and foil for other plants. It's very tough and happy in full sun and dry soils, although it doesn't like wet soils, where it tends to rot off. I keep my plants compact by cutting off the straggly pink flowers – in my book they detract from its beautiful foliage.

Roses
To save space I've used shrub roses and trained their stems like climbers.

Rosa Gertrude Jekyll (AGM)
Flowers: JULY–SEPTEMBER
Height/spread: 1.8M X 1M when trained to a wall or fence
With pink, silky corsages from summer through to autumn, this is a classic shrub rose for training as a small climber. One of the first to be bred by David Austin, Gertrude Jekyll has the heavy, long-lasting scent of old roses but without the susceptibility to black spot, mildew and rust. Plant roses so the knuckle where the stems meet the grafted rootstock is 6–10cm below the soil surface.

Rosa 'Strawberry Hill' as the buds burst in June.

Rosa Strawberry Hill

Flowers: Repeats through JUNE–SEPTEMBER
Height/spread: 1.2M X 2.5M if trained to a fence or wall

A new English shrub rose with sherbet-pink, cup-shaped flowers and a light, citrus scent, particularly in the morning. This rose has few thorns and is excellent for training on a fence in full sun. It also has lovely glossy green leaves and good disease resistance. It repeat-flowers through summer into autumn, so keep deadheading and tie in new stems to wires.

Shrubs and Climbers

Use to soften railings at the front of your house.

Clematis x *triternata*

'Rubromarginata' (AGM)
Flowers: JULY–SEPTEMBER
Height/spread: 6M X 2M

A pretty clematis with purple, propeller-shaped flowers that smell like hawthorn. It has a tidy habit making it a good choice for small front gardens. Plant deep so the bottom buds are covered with a hand's width of soil and add lots of compost and leafmould to the soil. Tilt the stems towards the support and protect from slugs. Cover the soil with a piece of slate or stone to keep the roots cool, and keep well watered through the growing season. As it's a late flowerer, prune this clematis in early spring to a couple of strong buds about 20cm above the ground.

Sambucus nigra f. *porphyrophylla* 'Eva'

(See page 52 for cultivation details.)

Cytisus battandieri (AGM)

Flowers: JUNE–JULY
Height/spread: 4M X 4M

Pineapple broom is a hardy, sun-loving shrub that looks its silvery best grown in the reflected heat of a south- or west-facing wall. Its laburnum-like, yellow flowers smell just like sugary pineapple cube sweets. It does well if you train it into a fan as this stops plants becoming leggy at the base. Trim back half of all new growth after flowering; never cut into old wood as it won't re-grow.

Elaeagnus 'Quicksilver' (AGM)
Flowers: MAY–JUNE
Height/spread: 4M X 4M
A small, deciduous and drought-tolerant tree with silvery, willow-like leaves and inconspicuous but heavenly scented cream flowers. It's far too big for a small front garden, but I've chosen to train it as a standard lollipop by clipping the foliage after it flowers (see page 89). Be careful not to damage its roots when weeding as it suckers (astrantia makes a good partner as it doesn't like being mucked about with either). It's ideal for city gardens where pollution is high, and also does well by the coast. the evergreen *Eleagnus x ebbingei* is better for chalky soils.

Lonicera periclymenum
'Graham Thomas' (AGM)
Flowers: JUNE–SEPTEMBER
Height/spread: 6M X 1.8M
A woodland honeysuckle with clusters of scented yellow bugles followed by (poisonous) jewel-red berries. Its scent is particularly sweet and pungent on warm, midsummer evenings. Pruning can be a bit of a pain, as this climber often grows into a tangled nest of stems. However, it's a tough plant so you can prune hard without any worry of doing permanent damage. Cut out spent shoots after flowering, leaving new growth to bloom next year. An excellent plant for bees, and useful for partly-shaded sites and east-facing boundaries.

Two self-seeding gap fillers; bronze fennel mingles with purple orache.

Your maintenance regime

If you complete these key seasonal tasks your scented scheme will go from strength to strength.

Spring

- Feed borders with a balanced fertiliser and mulch with garden compost as the crowns of herbaceous plants start to grow. Avoid fertilisers that have an unpleasant odour (chicken-manure pellets spring to mind) or you'll put off visitors!
- Tie the new growth of climbers to wire supports with loops of soft twine. Tying rose stems down horizontally is a good trick to encourage more flowers.
- Prune clematis in early spring before new growth sprouts; cut it 20cm from ground.

Summer

- Stake anthemis with peasticks if it starts to flop and trim back after the first flowers to encourage a second flush.
- Deadhead spent flowers from pinks and roses regularly.
- Cut down fennel when it starts to get leggy and sparse.
- Train and trim eleagnus as a standard (see page 89).
- Cut back wayward stems of the cytisus and tie in shoots you want to keep.
- Tie in roses as they grow.
- Take 10cm dianthus cuttings from non-flowering shoots and root in a pot of cuttings compost covered with a plastic bag.

Astrantia and the delicate umbels of *Sambucus* 'Eva'.

Deadhead repeat-flowering roses
for a long-lasting display.

Autumn

- Plant bulbs for early spring colour – tulips and alliums do not always come back for a second flowering, especially if there is dense shade at ground level, so in small spaces treat them as bedding and plant new ones every year.
- Lift, divide and replant perennials that are becoming overcrowded, freshening soil with compost.
- Trowel seedlings of lychnis and fennel to favourable positions.

Winter

- In November, plant up containers with lily bulbs; three to a 25cm pot.
- Remove stakes and spent flowers as they become untidy to make way for spring bulbs.
- Prune roses, snipping back side shoots to a few buds from the main stems. Remove any congested or poor-flowering old wood of established plants right down to the base to make way for fresh new growth.

A windowbox
recipe for sun.

Techniques for front gardens

The name of the game in restricted front gardens is packing in colour. Pots and pruning are key techniques.

Summer windowbox

This combination of flowers creates a classy, drought-tolerant scheme. I made my box from timber chopped from an old pallet of ready-made boxes but there are plenty, available to buy. Make sure there are drainage holes in the base and use a potting mix made from 50:50 multi-purpose and loam-based compost.

- *Elymus hispidus*: a striking plant with grassy silver foliage
- *Pelargonium sidoides*: a real winner, with plum-coloured flowers and silver leaves
- *Nemesia* and *calibrachoa*: this *nemesia* is scented, but any purple bedding with small flowers, including petunias or viola, will do

Training an eleagnus as a standard

Lollipop-shaped trees look lovely anywhere, but are especially useful in small spaces. The formal shape adds structure to the profusion of blooms, too.

1. Look at the tree and identify a strong, straight and, as near as possible, vertical branch to form the trunk of the tree. From mid-summer to mid-winter, use secateurs to cut back all the shoots that grow from the lowest third of the plant right back to the trunk. From the middle section, cut the shoots back to half of their length. It seems odd, but leaving the stubs encourages the stem to thicken to a solid trunk.

2. In autumn, when the plant is 1.2–1.5 metres tall, cut back the leader (the uppermost shoot) to a healthy bud or shoot, leaving four or five strong, well-placed lateral branches that will eventually form the framework of the lollipop. Any crossing or congested shoots should also be removed at this stage.

3. The following years, clip the crown to create a spherical shape after flowering and prune any poorly placed or congested branches and vertical shoots after leaf-fall.

How to build a cobble path

Cobble paths have timeless appeal and have proven their durability since Roman times. You don't need to be a master-builder to create one, although take time to ensure the finished level of the cobbles is above the surrounding soil. Alternatively, use timber edging to hold back soil and stop it falling onto the stones.

As a rough guide you'll need approximately 120kg of 60–120cm pebbles for every square metre of path, although this does depend on the average size of the cobbles. Order from a local stone supplier or a builders' merchant, who will also be able to supply the cement and sharp sand you will need. Sand is available in heavy but manoeuvrable 20kg bags, but if you're cobbling a large area it's far cheaper to buy the sand in tonne-bulk bags.

To cobble an area of one square metre you will need:
5 x 25kg bags of cobbles | 50kg cement |200kg sharp sand |Wheelbarrow |Lump hammer |Spade |Bucket |Trowel |Spirit level |Length of timber (for checking levels) |Gloves |Brush |Hosepipe with a spray attachment

1: Dig out the path to a depth of 10cm and compact the soil using a heavy lump hammer. Excavate an extra 10cm either side of your path to create a solid kerb that holds the sides of the path in place. As long as its top is below the path level it can be hidden with soil later.

2: Mix sharp sand and cement together in a wheelbarrow. Use four-parts sand to one of cement. Spread this dry mix along the bottom of the path roughly 75mm deep. You'll need enough to come just below the level of the surrounding soil.

3: Push the pebbles into the sand/cement mix. Put them flattest side down and tightly packed together, making sure at least half of every pebble is submerged in the mix. Aim to leave the top third of the pebbles above the surrounding soil. Wear gloves as cement is caustic.

4: Work in sections, checking for high spots by running a short length of timber over the pebble tops. Use a lump hammer on the timber to push down any high pebbles.

5: Add more cement and sand into the joints (this time mixed one-part cement to three-parts sand) so all but the top third of the pebbles are submerged. Brush off any residual cement from the tops of the cobbles.

6: Use the end of the mallet to press the cement into the sides of the path and reinforce the edges. Use a hose set to a fine mist to level the sand/cement mix. Leave for at least 48 hours before using the path. If it's your only means of access, put planks over the top to protect the surface while it hardens.

Ribbons of lavender and curry plant topped
with airy sprays of *Verbena bonariensis*.

4 | THE BANK

The Bank at Greenacre is a challenging place for plants. It's 20 metres wide, 6 metres deep, and covered with awful soil that can only be described as thin, stone-filled scree. To make things trickier, it faces east and has a 1:5 slope – it's such a difficult site that some weeds even struggle to grow! Thankfully there are shrubs and flowers that'll thrive even in a tricky situation like this one.

The starting point for any nutrient-poor bank is to establish lots of fast growers that will send down roots and bind the earth, preventing what little topsoil there is being washed down the slope by rain. I used a range of tough, Mediterranean shrubs with a tried-and-tested ability to grow in thin soils, and I planted them in wavy rows to bring a bit of uniformity and structure. These plants thrive in harsh conditions, although they still need planting with care to ensure they quickly become self-sustaining (see my planting guide on pages 102–3).

While the shrubs were establishing on one half of the bank, I decided to inject a splash of colour on the other. I sowed hard-working annuals and with spectacular results – perhaps the most successful was a great swathe of Californian poppies, which painted the slope vivid orange in summer.

Identify drought-tolerant plants
Some plants have evolved tricks that help them survive dry and exposed conditions, and often you can tell whether they're worth trying in a tricky situation just by looking at the leaves. Always look out for silver foliage as this reflects the sun and gets its colour from a hairy coat that covers the leaves.

In a nutshell: *this is an east-facing, 1:5 slope covered with tough, silver-leaved shrubs and hardy annuals*

Suited to: *this planting style is for you if you've run out of ideas for a dry and sun-baked, challenging site*

Ideal location: *an exposed slope, steep bank or nutrient-poor soil*

Space needed: *six square metres are adequate, although the bigger the area the more effective the planting will look*

Maintenance rating: *low. Keep on top of weeding; some pruning; annual seed-sowing*

Eco credentials: *good. Many of the plants I've used are welcome habitats for overwintering ladybirds and bees. They are also attractive to butterflies in summer*

Like an Arran jumper, this coat of plants slows the movement of air over the foliage, reducing the speed at which moisture is lost from the leaves. Also look for fragrant plants – the essential oils that give lavenders and helichrysum their characteristic aroma form a fug around foliage on hot days, again slowing the movement of air, and also detering pests. Other 'tough' characteristics include stiff waxy leaves (as on cistus), needle-shaped foliage, tiny leaves and wiry photosynthesising stems (as on broom).

Bank elements

Resilient Shrubs
Look to versatile shrubs and drought-tolerant Mediterranean evergreens for the backbone of your planting scheme.

Annuals
Direct-sow tough hardy annuals between young shrubs. They will bring welcome colour and suppress weeds.

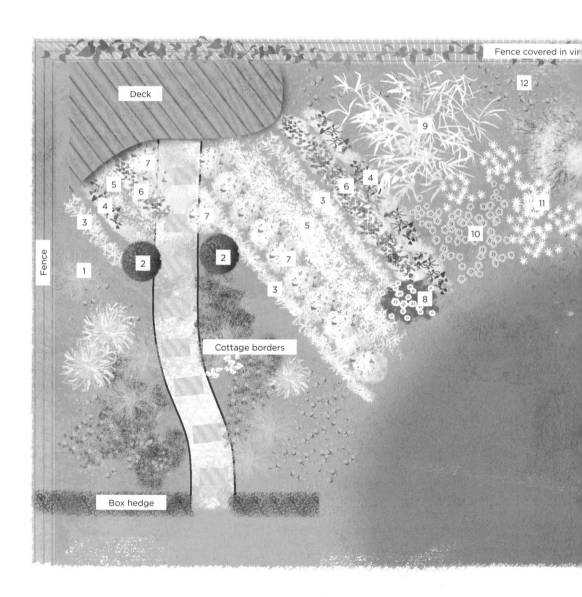

Rows

Planting shrubs in striking rows provides year-round structure and makes a slope look softer and less dominant. Growing plants with the same maintenance needs also makes for less work.

Mulch

Cover banks with mulch to suppress weeds and improve the soil. Mushroom compost or preparatory composted straw products are ideal as the mineralised and part-composted stems lock together, preventing weed growth. They also conserve moisture, add organic matter to improve soil, and don't slide downhill.

Green Manure

Direct-sow green manure, such as phacelia, in autumn. This will help stabilise the soil during winter rains, along with improving its nutrient content.

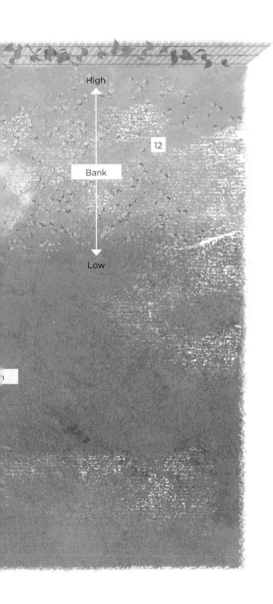

Verbena bonariensis and California poppies running throughout.

1: Buddleia
2: Box balls
3: *Helichrysum italicum*
4: *Lavandula stoechas*
5: *Artemisia* 'Powis Castle'
6: *Lavandula angustifolia* 'Munstead'
7: *Teucrium fruticans*
8: *Cistus* x *purpureus* 'Alan Fradd'
9: *Salix exigua*
10: *Halimium lasianthum*
11: *Senecio Cinearia* 'Silver Dust'
12: California poppies
13: *Genista aetnensis*

 N

My plant choices

Rather than dotting shrubs about randomly, I arranged the ones at Greenacre in waves of repeated lines, reminiscent of the lavender fields of Provence. They looked like separate hedges at first, but have started to knit together to create solid waves of foliage and summer flowers. We call it The Silver Sail, because when it was first designed it resembled an unfurled spinnaker.

Artemisia 'Powis Castle' (AGM)

Flowers: AUGUST

Height/spread: 60CM X 70CM

This is one of the best silver plants you can buy, with delicate, branching felt-covered leaves. There are a few forms of 'Powis Castle' about – some more silver than others – so look for the brightest when buying. Well-drained, fertile soil and a sunny position bring out the best colour. It won't tolerate heavy, or waterlogged soil.

Helichrysum italicum (AGM)

Flowers: JULY–AUGUST

Height/spread: 60CM X 70CM

The curry plant's leaves might smell like a chicken jalfrezi, but sadly they aren't edible. However, the plant's silver colour and ability to grow into a stocky hedge make it perfect for planting on a sunny bank. Like lavender, this plant needs sun and free-draining ground to thrive. It produces umbels of summer-born yellow daisies that complement lavender flowers perfectly.

Lavandula angustifolia 'Munstead'

Flowers: JULY–SEPTEMBER

Height/spread: 45CM X 60CM

A classic lavender that grows into a compact, aromatic, bushy shrub, with silvery grey-green leaves. 'Munstead' is available in blue and white forms and is prized by bees. It's slightly smaller than other cultivars, with neater leaves, making it a good choice for edging a path. Grow in fertile, well-drained to dry soil in full sun.

Lavandula stoechas (AGM)

Flowers: JUNE–AUGUST

Height/spread: 60CM X 60CM

French lavender is more flamboyant, slightly taller and less robust than its English cousin. It has more whorled, grey-green leaves, and its dark-purple flowers resemble tiny pine cones with two bracts sprouting out the top like bunny ears. Full sun and free-draining soil are a must.

Senecio cineraria 'Silver Dust' (AGM)

Flowers: JUNE–JULY although not grown for flowers

Height/spread: 30CM X 30CM

Silver senecio is a tender shrub usually grown for use in pots. Its oak-like leaves are covered in a silver down that gleams in bright sunshine, and I've used it on the bank as a stop gap to fill out the rows while permanent lavenders and artemisia are bulked up from cuttings. Raising large numbers from seed is easy and economical. Sow in March, plant out in sun and free-draining soil and they'll survive two, or sometimes three, winters.

California poppies thrive on poor, dry slopes and self-sow.

'California poppies emerge from pointy wizard hat buds on ferny silver-grey foliage'

Teucrium fruticans

Flowers: JUNE–AUGUST
Height/spread: 1M X 4M but 50/70cm when clipped

This plant's aromatic grey-green foliage forms a silver haze that is ideal for low, informal hedges and covering banks. It thrives in light soil and, given shelter from cold winds and plenty of sun, the leaves stay evergreen. *Teucrium* has delicate rosemary-like, pale-blue flowers and can be clipped to keep it small.

Backdrop shrubs

The backdrop for the Silver Sail comprises a range of robust shrubs including rock rose, wands of salix for winter interest, boulder-forming olearia and elegant 'Mount Etna' broom. They are all as resilient as the silver-leaved shrubs but add height and movement to the scheme.

Cistus x purpureus 'Alan Fradd'

Flowers: JUNE–JULY
Height/spread: 1M X 1M

The rock rose, with its leathery leaves, is a tough plant ideal for thin, chalky soil, dry banks or growing in the salt-laden air of a garden by the sea. It develops into a living boulder as it grows, and hunkers low to stay out of drying winds. Despite this apparent toughness, its flowers are as delicate as a field poppy, with soft, papery petals that tremble in the slightest breeze. 'Alan Fradd''s are white with burgundy blotches at the base. Each lasts just a day but they keep coming throughout the summer. Few other flowering plants will tolerate such tough, dry conditions. Grow in poor to moderately fertile soil in a sheltered, sunny site, planting after any risk of hard frosts has passed.

Genista aetnensis (AGM)

Flowers: JULY–AUGUST
Height/spread: 6M X 6M

This magnificent tree broom hails from the slopes of Mount Etna in Sicily. Its cascades of semi-weeping, whip-like branches erupt in masses of fragrant, golden-yellow, pea-like flowers. Grow in light, poor-to-moderately-fertile, well-drained soil in full sun.

Halimium lasianthum (AGM)

Flowers: JUNE–JULY
Height/spread: 1M X 1.5M

A close relative of cistus although, being from Portugal, it isn't quite as hardy. Its flowers are yellow, sometimes with a dark blotch at the base of each petal, which varies in size and colour from plant to plant. Shrubs have a loose, spreading habit, are reliable, hardy and flower for months. They have attractive silvery foliage, and thrive in a well-drained, moderately fertile sandy soil in full sun. They also appreciate shelter from cold, drying winds where possible. *Halimium* flower best in long, hot summers and don't like to be moved once established.

Salix exigua

Flowers: it bears catkins in spring
Height/spread: 4M X 4M

A fantastic willow for a tricky situation. In its native America it grows in tidal estuaries and sandbars where the roots have to cope with being either bone dry or drowned. Of all the willows, S. *exigua* is particularly elegant with slender, shimmering silver leaves that flutter from upright rod-like stems. On a dry bank the colour of the foliage is particularly good, as the lack of moisture means the leaves stay small and develop the colour of polished platinum. This is a deciduous plant with bare winter stems that are incredibly useful for cutting and weaving into wigwams to support clematis and sweet peas. I love it!

For a splash of colour

I sowed annual Californian poppies and phacelia over a large section of the Bank to act as 'green manure', protecting and preventing the soil from being washed down-slope by heavy rain. For height I've also added purple *Verbena bonariensis*. The seed of these flowers will happily self-sow, creating effortless and chaotic colour amongst the regimented silver artemisia and lavender.

Eschscholzia californica (AGM)

Flowers: JUNE–SEPTEMBER
Height/spread: 30CM X 15CM

Cheery orange flowers emerge from pointy wizard-hat buds on ferny silver-grey foliage in summer. Sow in spring for flowers the same summer; this annual is a brilliant way of cheering bare or poor soil and copes even on shallow chalks. Expect it to self-seed and crop up about the place the following year.

Phacelia tanacetifolia

Flowers: JUNE–OCTOBER
Height/spread: 70CM X 45CM

A great plant for attracting bees, with unusual lavender-blue flowers. The flowers also attract aphid-eating lacewings and hoverflies. On flat ground, dig in the tops after flowering finishes to feed the soil – strim and use as a mulch or cut down and compost. Sow any time from March to June for summer flowers, or September for winter foliage cover.

Verbena bonariensis (AGM)

Flowers: JUNE–SEPTEMBER
Height/spread: 2m x 45cm

Tall and skinny, this self-seeding perennial grows in a tracery of intricately branching green stems and bears small, lilac-purple flowers. It's best planted throughout a border like a purple veil and makes a good foil for other blowsy blooms.

Your maintenance regime

Once established a scheme like this will need little tending. There are a few key tasks to keep on top of, though.

Spring
- Direct-sow annuals for a summer-colour hit (see opposite).
- Trim back straggly and dead growth on helichrysum, artemisia and lavender to create neat 20cm hummocks. Trim teucriums to 40cm – as long as the plants are young and there are green buds low on all of the stems they'll happily re-grow.
- Sow cineraria indoors as an economical gap-filler.

Summer
- Lightly trim young cistus plants after flowering to encourage them to bush out. Don't prune them too severely as they won't regenerate .
- Prune the genista if it's getting too large, although don't cut into old wood. You can also take semi-ripe cuttings, although take lots as they can be difficult to root .
- Trim lavenders after flowering, cutting into the foliage by 5cm. Treat teucrium, helichrysum and artemisia in the same way as this guarantees neat and bushy tops for winter and the stems that regrow make excellent cuttings.
- Take cuttings of silver-leaved plants as insurance against loss if the winter is cold or very wet (see page 73).
- Hoe between plants to eliminate weeds, although hand-weed around any flower seedlings so as not to disturb the roots.
- Regularly pinch off tips of senecio to encourage a fresh flush of bushy growth from the base.

Autumn
- Pot on cuttings taken in late summer. Do this when they start to put on bushy growth and roots appear through the bottom of the container. Keep them in a cold frame.
- Direct-sow phacelia seed in early autumn to cover large areas of bare soil and protect the surface from winter rain.

Winter
- Coppice the S. *exigua* every three years. This will maintain a height of around 3m and encourage colourful new growth. Use the cut stems as plant supports or weave into wigwams with hazel rods. If the stems of your salix blocks an ugly view, maintain its height by cutting out the oldest third of the stems every year.
- Clear the tops of annuals and verbena to the compost heap when they become untidy.

Techniques for growing on an incline

On flat ground you simply sprinkle seed where you want flowers to grow and leave nature to do the rest. On a slope it's different; if you sow straight onto freshly weeded soil any rain will wash the seeds together into ribbons or, if it's torrential, right to the bottom of the bank.

Sowing seeds on a slope

To remedy the problem, make shallow furrows with a garden hoe, dragging the blade across (never down) the bank to create ridges (1) that slow the movement of water and hold the seeds in place. With small seeds like California poppy, just sprinkle over your furrows, with larger seed, use the hoe to drag soil back over the seed and just cover it (2). It's a simple trick, but incredibly effective if you're gardening on a slope. I chose Californian poppies for the bank at Greenacre. They formed a dazzling carpet of orange during the summer and, come autumn, their spent stems protected other 'green manures' sown to protect the soil during winter.

1

2

How to plant Provençal style

This colourful planting scheme creates eye-catching stripes, and is perfect for a sunny slope or bank. It's nothing complicated, just a series of parallel hedges of five different shrubs: *Artemisia* 'Powis Castle' (AGM), *Helichrysum italicum* (AGM), *Lavandula angustifolia* 'Munstead', *Lavandula stoechas* (AGM) and *Teucrium fruticans*.

Planting in rows creates lovely, wave-like undulations and provides a different look depending on the viewpoint. From above the lines are perfectly straight, but from the side they follow the serpentine contours of the soil, curving and casting shadows like vines on a hilltop vineyard. Planted amongst the rows are self-seeded Californian poppies, pot marigolds and *Verbena bonariensis* (AGM). I also plugged a few gaps with seed-sown cineraria.

To fill an area of 9 square metres you will need:
7 *Artemisia* 'Powis Castle' (AGM) | 7 *Helichrysum italicum* (AGM) | 7 *Lavandula angustifolia* 'Munstead' | 7 *Lavandula stoechas* (AGM) | 6 *Teucrium fruticans*

And to fill gaps in the first year:
10 *cineraria* | 1 x packet Californian poppy seeds | 1 x pot marigold seeds | 5 *Verbena bonariensis* (AGM).

1: Clear the bank of all perennial weeds and incorporate as much soil improver as you can. Fix evenly-spaced string lines 60cm apart across your slope and position rows of plants against them. Do the longest, most prominent line first, as this will form a guide for the rest of the bank, making sure the shrubs are positioned at regular intervals. Plant one shrub at a time, by first digging a hole that is three to four times larger than its rootball. Fork in a spade-full of garden compost as you go.

2: Pour half a can of water into the bottom of the hole and allow it to drain away. While you wait, start digging the next hole.

3: Gently knock the plant from its pot, tease out any roots that are congested and sprinkle with mychorrizae granules. This will help the plant form a secondary root system, enabling it to cope better with the poor ground.

4: Plant the shrub in the hole and mould the soil into a crater above the root ball. This acts like a sump for catching rainfall and stops water running down the bank. Plant the rest of the shrubs in the same way. Water immediately after planting, and keep plants well watered through dry spells in the first summer. Follow the maintenance regime on page 98 to keep the display in tip-top shape.

Dicentra spectabilis is up and in flower by early May.

5 | THE WOODLAND GARDEN

Few gardeners are fortunate enough to own a bit of real woodland but, thanks to neighbouring fences and trees, many of us have gardens with enough shade to grow an array of beautiful woodland flowers. This is the case at Greenacre, and our Woodland Garden is situated between a fence and the cool, north-facing walls of the greenhouse, with a few burgeoning trees. The plot is rectangular, roughly 10m deep and 30m wide, but I've tried to make the shape look more natural with serpentine paths and curved beds

The tried-and-tested way to get the most from a shady garden is to emulate what happens in nature. Natural woodlands consist of layers of trees, shrubs and herbaceous flowers that grow at different heights and have evolved to thrive in each other's company. The large trees at the top dominate over an understorey of smaller trees and shrubs that thrive in the dappled light or have dark, chlorophyll-filled foliage to cope in the gloom. Around their feet the herbaceous layer covers the soil. At Greenacre this is made up of winter-flowering hellebores, lady's mantle, heucheras and lots of flowering bulbs.

While the 'layer' approach is perfect for a large, natural, wooded glade, other tricks are needed to give a small-garden copse authenticity and a long season of interest. The key is using a diverse range of not necessarily native plants along with evergreens to hold the scheme together in winter. I've found bamboo is particularly useful for this and, although not in the traditional pallet of woodland plants, it is the perfect fence-hiding evergreen. It also looks surprisingly good in a woodland setting. We also use a range of climbers that scramble up and soften the bare walls and fences and create a luxuriant woodland feel.

In a nutshell: *this planting style is perfect for gardens with semi- and fully shaded areas*

Suited to: *this style is for you if you have a garden crowded by neighbours' fences or shaded by deciduous trees*

Ideal location: *these plants do best in improved soil in shady sites and in the lee of trees. Good for clay soils*

Space needed: *you need a minimum of 12 square metres to create a glade*

Maintenance rating: *moderate. Lots to do in concentrated periods of autumn and winter*

Eco credentials: *excellent. Woodland settings attract hedgehogs, birds, frogs and toads, all of which are beneficial in the garden*

Bulbs throughout:
Cyclamen hederifolium on sunny
edges of the central glade
Sheets of daffs
Snowdrops
Wood anemones

Flowers:
1: *Indocalamus latifolius*
2: *Helleborus foetidus*
3: *Fargesia rufa*
4: *Polystichum setiferum*
5: *Clematis tangutica*
6: *Helleborus* x *hybridus*
7: *Digitalis purpurea*
     Excelsior Group
8: *Heuchera* 'Purple Petticoats'
9: *Dicentra spectabilis*
10: *Anemone* x *hybrida*
     'September Charm'
11: *Anemone nemorosa*
12: *Carex* 'Amazon Mist'
     Uncinia rubra
13: *Heuchera* 'Beaujolais'
14: *Epimedium* 'Amber Queen'
15: *Gentiana* 'Blue Silk'
16: *Clematis* 'Elizabeth'

Woodland Garden elements

Soil
Woodland dwellers love humus-rich woodsy soil. Unless your garden offers these conditions, it's essential to work in lots of organic matter in the form of garden compost, leafmould (see page 16), composted bark or bought soil improver. Do this before planting and apply a liberal mulch every year. Along with improving soil, mulch suppresses weeds, retains moisture and adds to the woodland feel.

Tree Canopy
Very little grows directly beneath large, leafy trees unless you lift the canopy to let in more light. Tackle small branches by sawing them off in short sections back to the collar – the raised ridge or bark by the trunk. Never

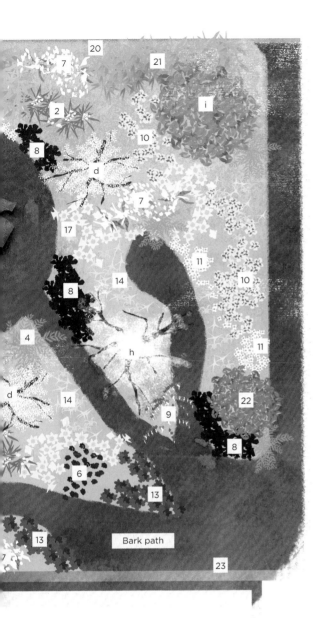

17: *Alchemilla mollis*

18: *Hosta* 'Sum and Substance'

19: *Phyllostachys aureosulcata*
    f. *spectabilis*

20: *Humulus lupulus* 'Aureus'

21: *Phyllostachys bissetii*

22: *Camellia* x *vernalis* 'Yuletide'

23: *Parthenocissus henryana*

24: *Chaenomeles speciosa* 'Nivalis'

Trees:

a: *Acer rubrum*
   ($1/10$ eventual size)

b: *Prunus* x *yedoensis*

c: *Acer palmatum* 'Osakazuki'

d: *Amelanchier lamarckii*

e: *Prunus* 'Kanzan'

f: *Acer davidii*

g: *Acer palmatum* var. *Dissectum*
   Atropurpureum Group

h: Prunus avium 'Plena'

i: *Cornus kousa* var. *chinensis*

N

leave stumps as they don't heal quickly or look natural. This trick also works with shrubs, too. Large branches are best left to tree surgeons.

Succession
Planting for year-round colour is key in a small woodland garden. I've organised my herbaceous plant choices by season to help you get it right.

Structure
Woodland flowers quickly come and go, so it's essential to use evergreens in key positions to hold the scheme together throughout the year. I chose to use heucheras, evergreen sedges and bamboo at Greenacre.

Landscape Materials

Use as many natural materials as possible. Sawn logs and woodchips make for easy and economical paths, while the large table and bench were made from a felled elm tree. The logs and chips were sourced from tree surgeons while the elm came from a local saw mill. We also buy bags of medium-grade bark chips to cover bare soil and create a neat cohesive look.

Style

Woodland plants colonise areas of light and shade, depending on their preference. Mimic this look by positioning herbaceous plants in pools and drifts. Use the opportunity to life and divide both bulbs and herbaceous plants to create that archetypal carpet effect of a woodland floor in bloom. And don't worry about keeping your woodland garden too tidy – fallen leaves, debris and piles of logs all add to the charm and encourage beneficial wildlife and hibernating hedgehogs.

Mix native and non-native

The way to get a natural look is more about how you plant than which you use – provided they suit the situation – so don't be strict about only using native woodland plants.

Thin out old canes of bamboo in winter by cutting to the ground with loppers.

My plant choices

Woodland gardens traditionally peak in spring but my aim was to have colour throughout the year. No trees are included in my selection, I've concentrated on the understorey as a solution to already existing shade.

Bamboo

Take note of whether a bamboo is a clump-former or a runner. Runners need room to spread or must be contained in some way. One option is to create a non-degradable barrier at planting time, which should be at least 60cm deep. We use heavy-duty polythene at Greenacre, normally sold at builders' merchants as damp-proof membrane. My selections all prefer a woodsy soil, so add leafmould or compost at planting time. Regular watering and shelter is key to establishment.

Fargesia rufa (clump-former)
Height/spread: 2M X 3M
A choice new introduction that's perfect for small gardens, and grows well in a pot. The culm sheaths and branches are tinted rusty orange-red to dusky pink – the more alkaline the soil, the pinker they get. The leaves are narrow and glossy with a blue-green glow, giving a distinctive, refined look. We have two plants at Greenacre that stand sentry either side of the path.

Indocalamus latifolius (runner)
Height/spread: 2M X indefinite
Slender and upright with handsome broad leaves held horizontally from the culms. New shoots are red. We have one plant at Greeenacre, which we'll divide in time to make a rustling grove. It's a good screening plant if you have noisy neighbours!

Phyllostachys aureosulcata f. spectabilis (AGM – runner)
Height/spread: 3M X indefinite
This is a large, showy bamboo with rich-green foliage and thick, yellow canes. It makes a loose clump with occasional runners and performs best in some sun. It's a great plant for children to hide in as the clumps are ideal for den building. We have a large plant to grow as a single specimen.

Phyllostachys bissetii (runner)
Height/spread: 5M X indefinite
One of the best bamboos for withstanding cold British winters, and also very good for screening. It remains green and lush throughout the year with masses of attractive foliage on strong, thick, green culms.

Bulbs and Corms

Plant in quantity and in swathes for the most natural look.

Anemone nemorosa (AGM)
Flowers: MARCH–APRIL
Height/spread: 15CM X 15CM
Once established this delicate perennial spreads into constellations of white, star-like flowers, often flushed pink. It's hardy and likes moist, well-drained, humus-rich soil in part-shade. It will grow among the roots of birch trees as it tolerates dry conditions when it's dormant in the summer.

Cyclamen hederifolium (AGM)
Flowers: SEPTEMBER–OCTOBER
Height/spread: 10CM X 15CM

Cyclamen love free-draining soil and do really well among the roots of trees. Plants grow from a corm, producing flowers first, followed by marbled, ivy-like leaves. They provide good evergreen cover through winter. The flowers coil back down to the ground when they're spent, taking seed with them that will gradually be spread by ants that love their sticky sugary coats to all parts of your garden. Cyclamen look best in big swathes, so plant corms in bulk from the outset.

Galanthus nivalis (AGM)

Flowers: FEBRUARY–MARCH
Height/spread: 15CM X 8CM

Vigorous and easy to grow, snowdrops are just the thing for naturalising. They look magical growing as a dense white carpet weaving between trees. Each bulb produces a single dangling bloom on an arching, slender stem – they melt the heart as they poke their dainty heads out through even the heaviest snow. There are hundreds of different varieties, each with different petal markings, to choose from. They like some shade and grow best in humus-rich, well-drained soil that doesn't dry out in summer.

Narcissus (for several months of colour)

I planted a range of narcissus to add colour and fragrance to the Woodland Garden from mid-winter right through to late May. The best ones for woodland are the more natural-looking, delicate species, including jonquils, tazetta, and cyclamineus, along with our native *Narcissus pseudonarcissus* (AGM). Daffodils make excellent cut flowers.

N. 'Actaea' (AGM)
Flowers: MAY
Height / bulb spacing: 45CM / 16CM

A 'poeticus' division daffodil with solitary scented flowers. The pure-white outer perianth spreads wide to frame small red-rimmed cups (coronas) inside.

N. 'Cheerfulness' (AGM)
Flowers: APRIL
Height / bulb spacing: 40CM / 16CM

A double-flowered daffodil with one or more flowers per stem, often with double outer perianth or corona.

N. 'Dutch Master' (AGM)
Flowers: APRIL–MAY
Height / bulb spacing: 45CM /8– 16CM

Bears golden yellow trumpets in mid-spring.

N. Jonquilla (AGM)
Flowers: MARCH–APRIL
Height / bulb spacing: 30CM / 5–8CM

A wild species daffodil from sunny Spain.

Mix daffodil varieties to have flowers right through from January to May.

It bears heads of up to five strongly scented golden-yellow flowers with small, pointy, outer perianth petals and tiny flat cups.

N. 'Minnow'
Flowers: MARCH
Height / bulb spacing: 18CM / 8CM
A dwarf variety, 'tazetta' division daffodil producing up to 20 flowers on stout stems with wide leaves. Usually scented.

N. Poeticus var. recurvus (AGM)
Flowers: APRIL
Height / bulb spacing: 35CM / 5–8CM
Thin, erect, strap-like leaves and white, single flowers with recurved petals and red-rimmed, yellow cups in late spring.

N. 'Quail'
Flowers: APRIL
Height / bulb spacing: 40CM / 8CM
Ideal as a cut flower thanks to its scented blooms. As a 'jonquilla' daffodil, each stem produces 1–5 flowers with a spreading outer perianth in mid- and late spring.

N. 'Rijnveld's Early Sensation' (AGM)
Flowers: JANUARY
Height / bulb spacing: 25–30CM / 8–16CM
A single trumpet-flowered variety.

N. 'Spellbinder' (AGM)
Flowers: APRIL
Height / bulb spacing: 50CM / 8–16CM
Bears sulphur-yellow trumpet flowers whose coronas usually fade to white.

Mulch around hellebores to show off saucer-shaped flowers and encourage self-seeding.

N.'Trena' (AGM)
Flowers: MARCH–APRIL
Height / bulb spacing: 30CM / 8CM
Solitary flowers are acutely angled to the stem, while the white outer perianth seems to fold back on itself, framing the slender, lemon-yellow, trumpet-shaped corona. Graceful and long lasting.

Herbaceous Plants and Shrubs

Create a scheme to provide colour and interest in every season.

Polystichum setiferum

'Herrenhausen' (AGM)
Height/spread: 70CM X 90CM
A dark evergreen fern which looks fresh and tidy for most of the year. It prefers most-day shade and a woodsy soil that doesn't sit too wet or dry at the extremes of the season. Plant as an accent on corners of the border with enough space between neighbours to show off its lacy arching fronds.

Spring and summer

Alchemilla mollis (AGM)

Flowers: JUNE–SEPTEMBER
Height/spread: 50CM X 60CM
A delightful, low-growing plant – see page 192 for details.

Chaenomeles speciosa 'Nivalis'

Flowers: MARCH–MAY
Height/spread: 2.5M X 5M
A lovely low-growing shrub that's ideal as a bush or trained against a fence. It's shade tolerant so it's perfect for growing flat against a house wall or underneath a north-facing bay window. Snowy white spring flowers are followed by golden quince fruit.

Dicentra spectabilis (AGM)

Flowers: APRIL–MAY
Height/spread: 90CM X 45CM
This plant disappears after its pink and white heart-shaped flowers have gone over, so share the spot with late starters like late-flowering anemones. Plants thrive in light shade and fertile soil, but will tolerate full sun if the soil stays moist. Their fleshy, fang-like roots are brittle and resent being fiddled with, so don't tease them out at planting.

Digitalis purpurea Excelsior Group (AGM)

Flowers: JUNE–JULY
Height/spread: 2M X 60CM
This wonderful group of foxgloves grows in multi-coloured drifts that I allow to freely self-seed. Any freebie seedlings can be dug up during the autumn, potted on and kept over winter in a cold frame for planting out the following spring. As a rule the lighter and more furry the foliage, the paler the flowers. Blooms come in pastel shades of creamy yellow, white, purple or pink and bees love them for pollen.

Hosta 'Sum and Substance' (AGM)

Flowers: JULY–AUGUST
Height/spread: 75CM X 1.2M
This beauty is unusual for a hosta as it does well in an open spot – the more light, more yellowy-green its heart-shaped foliage becomes – providing the soil is moist. It's less prone to slug and snail attack than some hostas as the leaves are so thick and leathery, but you still need to be vigilant.

Autumn

Anemone x hybrida
'September Charm' (AGM)
Flowers: AUGUST–OCTOBER
Height/spread: 1.2M X indefinite
This reliable anemone has soft, hairy leaves topped with solitary pale pink flowers cased in purple buds. It likes a moist, fertile and humus-rich soil in sun or a little shade, but won't tolerate much winter wet. This plant can take a while to establish but, if you're lucky, can almost become invasive. It's ideal for late-season colour underneath trees.

Anemone x hybrida
'Honorine Jobert' (AGM)
Flowers: AUGUST–OCTOBER
Height/spread: 1.2M X 1.5M

This is my favourite anemone, with soft hairy leaves topped with solitary white flowers only tinged pink on the reverse, and golden yellow stamens. It prefers a moist, fertile humus-rich soil in sun or part-shade but won't tolerate much winter wet. It's ideal for late season colour. Takes a while to establis.

Camellia x vernalis 'Yuletide'
Flowers: NOVEMBER–DECEMBER
Height/spread: 5M X 4M
A long-lived, evergreen shrub with dark, glossy green leaves. It bears small, brilliant-red, single flowers with golden anthers in autumn and winter – reminiscent of a hellebore. It needs consistently moist, mildly acidic soil – it does well in a pot as long as the roots don't dry out. It's one for sun and shelter on a woodland edge, where its buds will open one at a time in winter.

Plant daffodils in repeated swathes to link borders.

Gentiana 'Blue Silk'

Flowers: SEPTEMBER
Height/spread: 10CM X 25CM

An excellent plant with intense-blue, silky flowers at a time when there isn't a great deal else flowering. Most gentians have trailing stems each tipped with a large, trumpet-shaped flower, and like acid soil. The flowers are held upright on neat, compact plants.

Uncinia rubra

Flowers: JULY–AUGUST
Height/spread: 30CM X 35CM

An attractive sedge with dark-red to bronze-green leaves that intensify in colour through autumn. It does well in sun or part-shade in well-drained, moisture-retentive soil. It comes from mountainous and damp peaty places in New Zealand, and is evergreen, with dark-brown to black flower spikes. Keep its roots cool with a covering of mulch.

Winter

Carex 'Amazon Mist'

Flowers: not applicable
Height/spread: 30CM X 40CM

This pretty sedge has become more popular than C. comans 'Frosted Curls' as it holds its silver-green colour rather better. It's easy to grow from seed, too. It'll do best in sun or part-shade, although doesn't like it too damp as it has a tendency to rot off. It's good for softening the hard edges of paths and patios.

Helleborus foetidus (AGM)

Flowers: JANUARY–APRIL
Height/spread: 80CM X 45CM

This plant is commonly known as the stinking hellebore because its dark green leaves have a pungent, nutty smell if crushed. It's very pretty though, with pendent, bell-shaped green flowers with purple margins. This hellebore self-seeds freely and will tolerate dry shade once it's established. Good for a natural look.

Helleborus x hybridus

Flowers: FEBRUARY-APRIL
Height/spread: 45CM X 45CM

Although usually found growing in chalky or limestone soils, hybrid hellebores will tolerate a range of locations as long as they don't become waterlogged or battered by cold winds. This one is a striking deep purple but there are white and pink plants on marbled purple forms too. Keep separate sides of the garden if you want seedlings to stay true. Add lots of well-rotted leaf mould or organic matter to the soil and in damp situations plant on mounds raised 10cm or so above the surrounding soil level. A fabulous flower for the depths of winter – right when they're most wanted.

Spires of foxgloves.

Heuchera 'Beaujolais'
Flowers: MAY–JUNE
Height/spread: 30CM X 35CM

This has huge, evergreen, chameleon-like leaves which are burgundy and silver with deep-purple veins in shade and coral pink and silver in an open spot. It produces the best show of flowers of any heuchera – cream sprays on wiry 70cm tall stems.

Heuchera 'Purple Petticoats' (AGM)
Flowers: MAY–AUGUST
Height/spread: 40CM X 40CM

A fantastic plant with dark, scalloped leaves that have a purple, silky underside. Stems of cream flowers appear from late spring and the leaves become more frilly during winter, revealing more of their undersides. Grow in light, fertile, moist soil in sun or part-shade. Water with liquid fertiliser in summer to promote leafy growth and divide in spring.

Climbers

Climbers blur the boundary and add a whole new layer of colour without taking up much space. To grow them up trees, plant them 75cm away from the trunk and use twine to guide the growth towards it.

Clematis 'Elizabeth' (AGM)
Flowers: MAY–JUNE
Height/spread: 7M X 3M

Perfect for training over sheds, hiding fences and covering tree stumps. Flowers on the previous year's shoots and will grow in sun or shade as long as it's given shelter and well-drained soil. Leaves are purplish-green. Birds love to nest inside its tangle of stems. Flowers are pale-pink, last about a month and have a delicate almond scent.

Clematis tangutica
Flowers: JULY–OCTOBER
Height/spread: 6M X 2M

A vigorous clematis with abundant, yellow, bell-shaped blooms that turn into fluffy seedheads. Use it to cover a wall or train it into the canopy of a tree. This clematis grows best in moist, humus-rich soil with its roots in the shade and its top in full sun. Mulch in late winter with garden compost or well-rotted manure, avoiding the crown.

Humulus lupulus 'Aureus' (AGM)
Flowers: SEPTEMBER
Height/spread: 6M X 6M

A fragrant, twining perennial with rough, hairy stems and deeply lobed, golden-yellow leaves. Plant in moist but well-drained soil where the shoots can clamber up into the sun and develop the best colour. We allow ours to scramble through the hazel fence: it grows at an astonishing rate. The female inflorescences are used in brewing but they're just as good in dried-flower arrangements. Train yours over a fence or trellis for support and cut down to the ground like a herbaceous plant every winter.

Parthenocissus henryana (AGM)
Flowers: JUNE–AUGUST
Height/spread: 10M X 5M

A self-supporting climber that clings to walls and fences using sucker-like pads. Dark green, velvety, palmate leaves with silver-white veins in summer transform to a fiery red come autumn. Less vigorous than other Virginia creepers, it still needs space. It's useful for north-facing walls in small gardens. Trim back a third of the plant at planting to encourage new foliage.

Clematis will happily twine and self-cling along the weave of a hazel fence.

Your maintenance regime

For a successful woodland garden you need to keep on top of key tasks throughout the gardening year (although you can take a bit of a breather in the summer).

Spring
- Buy snowdrops 'in the green' and plant in clumps, 15cm deep, for flowers next winter.
- Lift and divide clumps of established snowdrops as soon as the leaves begin to die back.
- Chop back overgrown bamboo – you'll need a mattock and a saw to cut the tough roots.
- Lift and replant sprawling heucheras, burying stems with 5–10cm of soil to encourage new growth from the woody stems.
- Mulch around herbaceous plants to set off their leaves and to create a seed bed for the progeny of hellebores and foxgloves.
- Apply a top dressing of general fertiliser around hellebores.
- Split, divide and replant gentians in April, improving soil with compost.
- Collect seedlings of hellebores that sprout around the base of plants. Pot up or trowel to an open spot to grow on.
- Divide sedges to make more plants and freshen up old clumps.
- Be on constant watch for slugs and snails, a small amount of damage on an unfurling leaf is magnified tenfold once it opens.
- Scatter seed of foxgloves in May where you want them to flower next summer or sow in pots.
- Cut down leaves of narcissus if they look tatty at least six weeks after flowering .
- Water in dry spells.

Summer
- Remove spent seedheads and tired foliage from sedges, alchemilla and foxgloves.
- Prune back wayward stems of *Clematis* 'Elizabeth' (AGM) after it flowers.
- Dig up and pot on self-seeded foxgloves and keep them in a cold frame over winter.
- Feed camellias with a balanced liquid fertiliser if the leaves show signs of yellowing in June and July.

Autumn
- Plant drifts of narcissis in holes twice as deep as the height of the bulb.
- Plant wood anemones, soaking the corms for an hour beforehand to rehydrate.
- Rake fallen leaves from paths into borders for a neat look until all have fallen, avoiding piling them onto crowns of plants, or collect in bin bags and make into leafmould.
- Apply a generous mulch of well-rotted organic matter around hellebores.
- Don't let camellias dry out once buds form.

Winter
- Thin bamboo by snipping old tired canes to the ground. Wear gloves as the stubs can easily cut the back of your hand.
- Encourage new bamboo growth by feeding plants with fish, blood and bone and mulching.
- Mulch soil to create a backdrop for emerging bulbs and herbaceous foliage.
- Cut spent stems of golden hops down to the ground and tidy tired fern foliage.
- Cut back stems of *Clematis tangutica* to strong buds 20cm above ground level and remove the dead tops to the compost heap.
- Top up paths with bark.
- Trim back overgrown *Parthenocissus* from window frames and guttering.

Chandeliers of *Nectaroscardum siculum* in July.

Techniques for the Woodland Garden

Maintaining the Woodland Garden is largely about tidying blitzes in late spring and autumn, propagating plants and keeping borders well mulched – both to maintain the soil and to achieve that woodland look. Use a sprinkler to water in prolonged periods of drought.

Cutting back dead foliage

There are two good reasons for cutting back tired and dead foliage of herbaceous perennials in winter. Firstly to show off any imminent flowers, and secondly, to expose the fresh crowns and make way for mulching. With hellebores it is to cut away any leaves badly affected by hellebore leaf blotch, a disfiguring though not usually not fatal fungal disease.

1

2

Make a woodland path

I like to use timber logs as an edging for bark paths. It's easy and economical to source logs from local tree surgeons but another way is via www.coppice-products.co.uk, who can put you in touch with local woodland workers. Use a spade to dig out 10cm of earth where you want your path – curving serpentine lines look best – and spread earth into borders (before planting). Lay out logs along the path edge, butting ends together. Ram earth around them with the handle of a lump hammer to hold them in place and top up with a deep 5cm layer of bark or woodchips along the path.

How to camouflage your fences with rustic hazel

The thing that often gives the game away in urban woodland gardens is ugly fencing. It was the case at Greenacre, with the directors and cameramen always complaining about how our own fence backdrop dominated their shots. To remedy the problem I decided to cover the lot with woven hazel panels. Hazel panels are crafted from 1–3cm thick 'rods' (straight sticks of hazel) woven together to form a strong and dense barrier. They can be bespoke, but are readily available to buy as 1.8m squares for about £50 each. They'll last for around five years if left untreated and kept above the soil, longer if you treat them with linseed oil. I like them because they look the part and are easy for climbers to scramble through. They are also good for the environment as they're sourced from coppiced woodlands.

You will need:
Hazel panels | Drill | Wood drill bit | Vine eyes | 2mm plastic-wrapped wire

1: Drill three pilot holes spaced 60cm apart into each of your fence posts. Make sure the posts are in good, robust condition first.

2: Screw vine eyes into the holes and then prop up the hazel panels on bricks to hold them off the ground.

3: Lash the panels to the vine eyes with wire and, once secure, remove the bricks and keep soil brushed back from their base (this will prolong their life).

1

2

3

Choose natural materials for a woodsy look.

The Bedding Border
in spring.

6 THE BEDDING BORDERS

Bedding is full-on, massing together annuals, biennials, bulbs and tender perennials to create a colourful seasonal explosion. It involves year-round renewal to keep the colour coming, but it's worth it. The vast range of plants available means you can create any look you like, from a combination of soft and subtle pastel shades to a mix of bright and clashing blooms.

Traditional bedding seems to have gone out of favour in recent years, but I think the skill of producing a good display, formal or not, is something to be celebrated. Our parks used to be full of spectacular bedding schemes but sadly budget cuts mean these displays are becoming increasingly rare. If the tradition is to stay alive it's going to be down to us gardeners.

The spring bedding at Greenacre is fairly traditional, comprising wallflowers, tulips and euphorbia. The summer scheme is a modern interpretation of a Victorian display, incorporating tropical seed-sown castor-oil plants, along with houseplants, climbers used as ground cover and tender grasses. These plants can be a little expensive to buy, although you can keep them for years if you are prepared to lift them in the autumn and keep them in a frost-free place.

The two Bedding Borders are the most work-intensive beds we have at Greenacre, but I love them because they offer so much opportunity for creativity, plant planning and hands-on gardening. The borders are about 7m wide and 2m deep, and flank a grass path leading to the greenhouse. Walking between them when they're at their peak is a real pleasure as they punch well above their weight in terms of colour.

In a nutshell: *go for a bedding scheme for a seasonal blast of colour that can be changed from year to year, and season to season*

Suited to: *high-impact bedding is perfect in many situations, but in particularly front gardens and new borders where you are waiting for permanent planting to grow*

Ideal location: *fertile soil and a sunny spot are a must*

Space needed: *one square metre is enough for starters*

Maintenance rating: *high. You'll need to keep on top of year-round weeding, deadheading, feeding, watering and planting*

Eco credentials: *low–moderate. Avoid double flowers which are of little use to wildlife*

Bedding elements

Planning
There are no rules when it comes to bedding combinations, however, it's best to ensure your display looks cohesive and not just a jumble of flowers. One way is to plan ahead by snipping out pictures of different flowers you fancy from catalogues, and paste them into a collage stuck on a sheet of paper.

Height
Think of your scheme in a series of layers, with uniform ground cover, mid-height plants and taller things for the back. You can be more adventurous with summer bedding by adding taller 'dot plants' and single centrepieces.

Colour
Bright glossy colours make pastels look washed out and they rarely complement one another. Combine clashing colours, like pinks and oranges, by finding a tone they share.

Foliage
Combine plants with different foliage to create a tapestry effect, which knits together and creates a foil for the flowers. Usual suspects include silver cineraria and coleus for summer borders and ivy for winter schemes. I also like to experiment with unusual substitutes, including the sprawling wall shrub *Muehlenbeckia complexa* and the dark-leaved *Ipomoea batatas* 'Blackie'.

Repetition
Create the biggest splash by bringing together large numbers of a few plants, rather than a confusing medley of lots of different types.

The Bedding Border in summer: *Muehlenbeckia complexa* woven through borders.

1: *Tradescantia pallida*
2: *Tithonia rotundifolia*
3: *Colocasia esculenta* 'Black Magic'
4: *Ricinus communis*
5: *Canna*: 'Black Knight' and 'Wyoming'
6: *Ensete ventricosum* 'Maurelii'
7: *Colocasia esculenta*
8: *Pennisetum setaceum*

'Ballerina' and 'Barcelona' tulips steal the show in April.

My plant choices

Spring choices

The Greenacre spring-bedding scheme comprises a simple palette of just four plants: *Tulipa* 'Ballerina' (AGM), *Tulipa* 'Barcelona' (AGM), *Erysimum cheiri* 'Blood Red' and *Euphorbia polychroma* (AGM). They flower at the same time, providing coordinated colour from March to May. There's a mixture of maroon, lemon-yellow and lime, and the display also provides scent and cut flowers.

Producing this look is all down to planning. You need a minimum of six wallflowers, nine tulip bulbs of each variety and one or two euphorbias per square metre. Set out the wallflowers first, followed by the euphorbias towards the front, then interplant with tulips. Tulips are best planted late – in November – as this helps avoid the fungal disease tulip fire, which blotches and twists the leaves, so don't feel you need to plant everything on the same day. Our soil has a pH of 5.5, so adding mushroom compost helped raise the pH to get the best out of the lime-loving wallflowers.

Erysimum cheiri 'Blood Red'
Flowers: MARCH–MAY
Height/spread: 45CM X 30CM
Wallflowers are early-flowering fragrant biennials, useful for bedding out en masse to create a carpet of colour which binds the stems of spring bulbs together. 'Blood Red' is one of my favourites, a deep velvety-red and sweetly scented. I sow wallflowers from seed because you get strong plants and a wide range of colours to choose from. It takes a bit of planning, sowing in June,

spacing out in August and finally lifting and replanting in their final position in the autumn. We sow wallflowers in a spare bit of ground at Greenacre, although they do perfectly well sown in pots. All this moving might seem like a lot of work, but each time the plants are lifted their roots are cut, so they become more fibrous and better able to feed, resulting in bigger and more floriferous plants. For an easy life, you can buy bundles of bare-root wallflowers from greengrocers and nurseries in autumn. However, they never end up putting on as good a display as seed-sown plants, so need planting more closely, and the colour range is usually limited. Put plants on the compost heap when the display's over.

Euphorbia polychroma (AGM)

Flowers: APRIL–MAY
Height/spread: 40CM X 60CM
This clump-forming herbaceous perennial has bright yellow flowerheads and bracts and is a perfect partner for tulips. We have plants that are used for spring bedding and then dug

up and replanted elsewhere for the summer. We use them again come autumn when the spring scheme is planted out. It's usually possible to divide plants every year, and seed germinates reliably if sown in autumn and left in a cold frame over winter. Stake plants in the summer to stop them falling apart, leaving a bare, open centre.

Tulipa 'Ballerina' (AGM)

Flowers: APRIL–MAY
Height/spread: 50CM X 10CM

A lily-flowered tulip that bears gracefully splayed flowers in a vivid tangerine-orange, with pink flames licking up its petals. Flowers appear in late spring and give off a heady fragrance in sunny weather. Plant bulbs 15–20cm deep in a fertile, well-drained soil in full sun from late October onwards. Remove faded flowers but don't cut back the stems before autumn. Lift bulbs and store them in a dry shed until you're ready to plant them again in autumn –see page 137 for details.

Tulipa 'Barcelona' (AGM)

Flowers: MAY
Height/spread: 50CM X 10CM

'Barcelona' is a Triumph tulip so it flowers in May, is good in rough weather and is a sturdy, traditional goblet shape. The blooms are fuchsia pink, and appear to glow when they're backlit by the sun. Grow in the same way as 'Ballerina'.

Summer choices

The summer scheme at Greenacre is vibrant and informal, very unlike the regimented park-department schemes of old. However, it requires the same loving care and attention to detail. It has a distinctly tropical flavour, relying largely on the extravagant foliage of canna lilies, bananas and colocasia. These are shot through with the citrus shades of more traditional seed-sown bedding, including gazania and tithonia. The beauty of this scheme is that the majority of the plants can be kept from year to year, provided they are lifted and kept frost-free over winter. Your scheme can stay the same each summer or you can experiment with new combinations by varying your sowing choices every year.

Canna 'Black Knight'

Flowers: JULY UNTIL FROSTS
Height/spread: 1.8M X 50CM

This exotic perennial looks a bit like a gladioli on steroids, with striking bronze foliage and large, dark velvet-red flowers. There's nothing subtle about cannas and their flowers are massive (often 8cm across), with wavy-edged petals in jungle-vibrant colours. 'Black Knight' is one of the most dramatic cannas you can buy, and its rich and vibrant colouring would stand out in the deepest, darkest depths of a tropical rainforest. Cannas thrive in a fertile, sheltered position in full sun, although they are damaged by frost and need winter protection. If you can't face the faff of lifting cannas every autumn, grow one in a container on the patio and bring it into a porch or cool conservatory instead.

Canna 'Wyoming' (AGM)

Flowers: JULY UNTIL FROSTS
Height/spread: 1.8M X 50CM

Yellow-flowered 'Wyoming' forms a vibrant focal point amongst deep greens and darker reds, purples and blacks. Its huge, brown-and-purple-veined leaves are joined by enormous, frilly-edged blooms on long stalks. Grow in the same way as 'Black Knight'.

Colocasia esculenta

Flowers: not applicable
Height/spread: 1.5M X 1.5M

Colocasia, or taro as it's sometimes known, is found in tropical swamps and is traditionally grown for its edible tubers and leaves, both of which must be cooked before eating. Here in Britain, colocasia is grown for its huge, spectacular, heart-shaped leaves, which bring instant tropical scale. Plant them in full sun or part-shade and water regularly – constant moisture is the key to success. This variety has green arrow-shaped leaves and stems, and is comparatively hardy as colocasias go – some gardeners even leave it in the ground under a layer of mulch during winter. It's too cold for that at Greenacre, so we lift colocasias in autumn and keep them under cover in winter. Treat colocasia tubers like dahlias, potting them up in March and planting out after the last spring frosts. Colocasia sap may irritate your skin so wear gloves if you ever need to cut into it.

Colocasia esculenta 'Black Magic'

Flowers: not applicable
Height/spread: 1.5M X 1M

'Black Magic' has dark purple, almost black leaves and stems and should be grown in

Wispy flower-heads of *pennisetum* in high summer.

the same way as straight esculenta. It's less hardy, though, so wherever you live you'll need to bring it indoors over winter.

Ensete ventricosum 'Maurelii'

Flowers: not applicable
Height/spread: 2.5M X 2.5M

The ultimate bedding plant, this ensete is very fast-growing, producing huge paddle-shaped leaves, which are olive-green with splashes of red and a deep red midrib. Ensetes have very fibrous roots, which means they tolerate being planted outside for the summer and then dug up and brought inside for the winter. Start to feed

plants with a balanced liquid fertiliser in March, in readiness for planting out after the last spring frosts. (Read more about ensetes in the Exotic Garden chapter, starting on page 202.)

Muehlenbeckia complexa

Flowers: AUGUST–SEPTEMBER
Height/spread: 3M X 6M (against a wall)

This evergreen plant originates from rocky areas of New Zealand. Tiny, star-shaped, greenish-white and sweet-scented flowers accompany its rounded, dark green leaves at the end of summer. I use it as a vigorous, twining climber/scrambler because it has small leaves that contrast well with the bold shapes of its neighbours. When grown against a sheltered wall it retains most of its leaves over winter, however it will lose them in cold, exposed sites (sow as for *Pennisetum villosrum* – see page 152 for details).

Pennisetum setaceum (AGM)

Flowers: JULY–SEPTEMBER
Height/spread: 80CM X 60CM

This clump-forming grass is found growing wild in savannah and woodland environments. Here in British gardens it's cultivated for its feathery spikes in summer and autumn, providing texture and movement for any summer bedding scheme. It's less hardy than most pennisetums (-5°C is its absolute limit), although it is very easy to grow from seed.

Ricinus communis

Flowers: JULY–SEPTEMBER
Height/spread: 1.8M X 1M

The castor-oil plant is a fast-growing, evergreen that hails from Africa and Asia. In its tropical homeland ricinus grows into a tree reaching 8–12 metres high, but in Britain it is grown as a dramatic foliage plant to provide a summer highlight. I use it at the back of the Greenacre borders to form a shaggy curtain of leaves. All parts of this plant are poisonous, with the seeds being particularly toxic. Start plants off from seed (see maintenance regime) and grow in moist, well-drained soil, sheltered from winds.

Tithonia rotundifolia 'Torch'

Flowers: JULY–OCTOBER
Height/spread: 1.8M X 70CM

Though not too commonly grown, this Mexican showstopper is a useful plant for adding height to displays with its erect, stout-stemmed flowers. Its bright orange, daisy-like flowers are extremely striking and last well when cut. Once planted in the ground it's a really fast grower, although it can be a bit of a malingerer in a pot in the greenhouse until the heat of summer arrives.

Tradescantia pallida

Flowers: CONTINUOUSLY IN
A GOOD SUMMER
Height/spread: 30CM X 40CM

This trailing, evergreen perennial (a species of spiderwort) has rich, violet-purple leaves and upright purple stems bearing pink flowers. The perfect foil for bright reds and oranges, its tender, and best known as a houseplant, but makes for glamourous ground cover outdoors. It needs to be acclimatised to full sun by hardening off over three weeks in spring. Divide clumps in spring to take stem-tip cuttings, rooting them in gritty compost on a heated potting bench.

Pennisetum sits at the feet of torch flowers, canna lilies and castor oil leaves

Your maintenance regime

You need your eye on the ball to pull a cracking bedding display out of the bag, keeping on top of essential, year-round tasks.

Spring
- Watch out for aphids on tulips and spray with a mineral soap to keep them at bay.
- Stake wallflowers with peasticks if necessary.
- Pot up canna rhizomes into multi-purpose compost and gradually increase watering to bring them into growth. Grow on under glass and protect from frost.
- Pot up colocasia tubers (concentric rings up, flattened side down) 15cm deep in multi-purpose compost. Grow on under glass and protect from frost.
- Sow ricinus seeds in late March. Soak them in tepid water for a few hours first, grow on under glass and protect from frost .
- Sow tithonia seed at 18–21°C in late March. Grow on under glass and protect from frost.
- Take tip cuttings of tradescantia in spring – they root easily in water or compost.
- Buy banana plants in small pots in spring or grow from seed in a propagator set to 25°C. Seed-sown plants will be big enough to use in your bedding scheme in their second year.
- Buy containerised pots of muehlenbeckia and take nodal cuttings to bulk up numbers.
- Place spent wallflowers on the compost heap and lift and replant euphorbia elsewhere.

Summer
- Clear the ground of spring bedding. Dig up and dry off tulip bulbs and store in a cool, dry place ready for replanting in late autumn. Leave euphorbia in place or lift, divide (if crowns are 15cm across) and replant it elsewhere in the garden.
- Rejuvenate your soil by incorporating lots of well-rotted manure/compost and watering well.
- Plant out your summer scheme once the last spring frosts have passed. Mulch with compost to keep the soil moist and to suppress weeds.
- Protect plants from marauding slugs and snails with wildlife-friendly pellets, traps or baits.
- Keep on top of watering. Plants with large leaves (canna, ensete and colocasia) need plenty of water throughout the growing season.
- Feed hungry plants regularly. Colocasias and cannas are particularly greedy, so give them a liquid feed once a week over the summer and apply pelleted chicken manure at planting.
- Deadhead all plants regularly to encourage more flowers. Ricinus seeds are highly toxic, it's a good idea to deadhead it before the seeds set if you've got pets or young children.
- Trim back tradescantia if plants become leggy or invasive and take root tip cuttings to make new plants.
- Sow wallflowers for spring bedding schemes in June.

Autumn
- Plant July-sown wallflowers in September–October, spacing out six plants per square metre, and one or two euphorbia. Water well after planting.

- Look out for signs of yellow streak virus on cannas. It's a spreading disease that starts as pale lines along the veins and then as holes where affected cells die. Burn or compost affected plants but save the seed which is free of the disease.
- Sow seed of cannas in a propagator set to 21°C and over winter in warmth (a conservatory or porch). They'll be large enough to put on a show next year.
- Lift healthy canna and colcocasia rhizomes and store in a barely moist multi-purpose compost or leafmould in a frost-free place. Trim back any tatty leaves but be careful of the colocasia, as it is a skin irritant.
- Dig up the tradescantia before the first frosts. Trim back plants, pot up and overwinter in a heated greenhouse or indoors as houseplants.
- Lift and trim the muelhenbeckia to 1.8m. Pot it up and keep it in a sheltered spot outdoors.
- Dig up and pot on the pennisetum and keep it in a cold greenhouse over winter.
- Discard the ricinus or grow it on as a small conservatory shrub.
- Dig up the ensete and keep it in a warm greenhouse (or use as a houseplant) over winter.
- Collect seed from *Pennisetum setaceum* (AGM) in early autumn and sow in compost-filled trays placed in a propagator.
- In late October or November, add tulips, planting bulbs 15–20cm deep and spacing them nine per square metre.
- Before the first severe frosts hit, dig up canna and dahlia for drying off and storing as dormant roots over winter. Some plants need to be potted up and kept growing in a frost-free greenhouse or conservatory, including colocasia, tradescantia and ensete.
- Condition your soil and plant out your spring scheme. Wait until November to plant tulips and be careful when planting euphorbia – the milky sap is toxic and can be a skin irritant.

Winter
- Ventilate overwintering plants on warm days to reduce the risk of fungal infections. Also remove and compost leaves that become tired and tatty.
- Keep an eye on your spring scheme, firming plants into place if they become lifted by frost.

The silver foliage of *Cineraria* 'Silver dust' makes a great filler.

Techniques for the Bedding Border

The skill of creating a great spring and summer bedding scheme comes down to renewal: planting up your spring bedding scheme in autumn, then in late spring, lifting plants that are past their prime to make way for flowers that will light up the summer ahead.

Storing tulips in late spring

Deadhead tulip flowers as they fade then, as soon as tulip flowers go over, lift and store the bulbs ready for replanting the following year. Push a spade down into the soil 10cm behind the bulb so when you lever back on the handle it's the soil around the bulb and not the hard blade that brings it to the surface (1). Pack by variety in boxes and leave in a greenhouse (2). When the tops become paper-dry, snip off with secateurs above the bulb and store in bags in a cool, dry place.

1

2

Planting the summer bedding scheme

Prepare a few weeks beforehand by hardening off plants grown in the greenhouse. After the risk of late frosts is over (late May/early June depending on where you live) pick a warm, dry day to improve the soil with compost or manure and rake flat. Set out plants on the soil before planting, grouping low-growers together in drifts and using large plants as single specimens. Water pots before planting and again once they are in the ground to settle soil around the roots. Always protect newly-planted bedding with a scattering of organic slug pellets and place fleece over plants for the night should another frost be forecast.

How to move tender plants for winter

To make large specimens, such as ensetes, more manageable, trim away the lower leaves first. Dig a trench around the roots 50cm away from the stem (1), then lever the plant to the surface with a spade. If it's too heavy to lift, tickle away some of the soil with a hand fork to reduce the weight and pot up using fresh potting compost into containers just wider than the roots (2 and 3). Move to a heated greenhouse or porch with a minimum winter temperature of 5°C (4) and water sparingly to just keep the plants ticking over. From early spring, increase the irrigation and encourage new growth with a fortnightly feed of tomato fertiliser.

Eupatorium and *persicaria* complement the sun-bleached seedheads of ornamental grasses in late summer.

7 | THE MODERN PRAIRIE BORDER

If I'm honest I don't like the name Prairie Border; it sounds irrelevant unless you have a garden the size of the Great Plains of North America. I do, however, like the style. It started life in Europe in the 1990s and was pioneered by the Dutch garden designer Piet Oudolf. He experimented by using ornamental grasses and perennials to cover large areas in public parks, creating colourful, wildlife-friendly and low-maintenance landscapes.

Gardeners quickly cottoned on, and started to exchange high-maintenance delphiniums for swaying grasses interspersed with drifts of gorgeous self-supporting perennials, including starry asters, echinacea and the vivid trumpets of daylilies.

Our Prairie Border is roughly 5 metres square and situated at the centre of the garden. Unlike many herbaceous borders, which peter out in late summer, it gets better through the heat of July and August, building to a crescendo of colour in late September. Even then the show doesn't stop; as flowers fade, their spent stems and the seed-heavy heads look beautiful, glowing in the low sun and catching the frosts and cobs of autumn. Best of all, we managed to propagate enough material from the plants in just one summer to develop another area of the same size for free.

Many of the plants used in prairie schemes are from North American prairies and can naturally cope with being planted close. In fact, crowding perennials and grasses of a similar height cheek-by-jowl smothers out weeds and eliminates the need for staking. Of course, you don't have to use just American natives – any perennial or ornamental grass that does well in your garden can be added to make the look your own.

In a nutshell: *this is a relaxed scheme with drifts of ornamental grasses and perennials*

Suited to: *this planting style's for you if you prefer grasses to shrubs and an informal look*

Ideal location: *an area with well-drained soil and plenty of sun is perfect*

Space needed: *a minimum of three square metres is ideal, although the larger the area the more natural it will look*

Maintenance rating: *low. You'll need to do a blitz once or twice a year*

Eco credentials: *excellent. The plants in this border are high in pollen and nectar, which attract beneficial insects, and seedheads that are magnets for birds*

Dotted throughout with
Allium caeruleum and
Nectaroscordum siculum.

1: *Sedum* (Herbstfreude
   Group) 'Herbstfreude'
2: *Bouteloua gracilis*
   or *Pennisetum
   alopecuroides*
   'Hameln'
3: *Aster* 'Little Carlow'
4: *Persicaria amplexicaulis*
   'Firedance' or 'Rosea'
5: *Rudbeckia fulgida* var.
   deamii
6: *Sedum* 'Red Cauli'
7: *Echinacea purpurea*
   'Rubinstern'
8: *Helenium* 'Sahin's Early
   Flowerer' or *Echinops
   ritro* 'Veitch's Blue'
9: *Calamagrostis*
   x *acutiflora*
   'Karl Foerster'
10: *Panicum virgatum*
   'Heavy Metal'
11: *Eupatorium purpureum*
12: *Miscanthus sinensis*
   'Abundance'
13: *Miscanthus sinensis*
   'Yakushima Dwarf'
14: *Helianthus*
   'Lemon Queen'

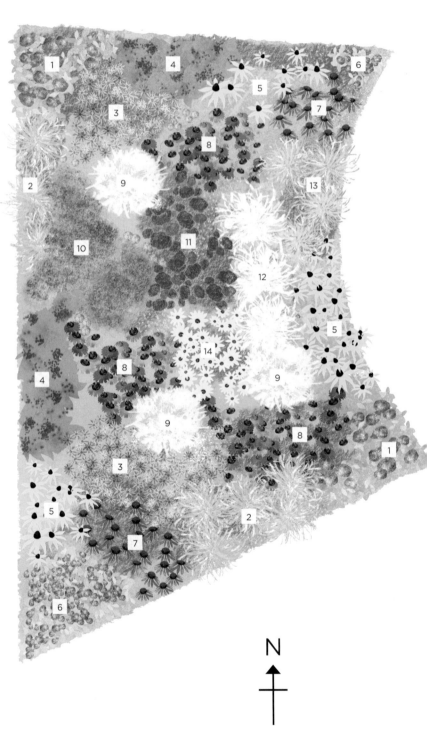

N

Prairie border elements

Sun

The one thing all prairie plants need is sun. They won't produce a good display without it and your scheme will end up looking like a damp squib. For me, a prairie that's backlit at some time of the day is also essential – sun shining through stems transforms a border into a sparkling, flower-filled field of gold.

Soil

Prairie perennials and grasses will grow happily in an ordinary unimproved soil, but it's essential that it's well-drained. With heavy soils improve drainage by adding compost to improve the texture and encourage worms to keep soil aerated. An early summer mulch will help too.

Quantity

The idea is to replicate nature, so planting large groups of the same species is what's needed to create the effect. For colour and impact, repeat the same variety more than once across the border.

Propagation

Buying large numbers of the same plant is often unappealing and can seem both boring and expensive. However, prairie plants, especially grasses, spread quickly and are easy to bulk up from seed and division (see page 154–5) so you'll easily be able to boost your stock.

Height

Substitute tall plants like eupatorium and miscanthus for shrubs to create high points amongst groups of low-growers.

Texture

Neighbour groups of plants with different shapes and textures. For example, plant 'round' daisies next to 'spiky' pokers or persicaria.

Access

If you're planting a large area (deeper than 5m) run a path through the middle to make tending easier. Our prairie border is completely surrounded by paths on all sides.

Sedum 'Red Cauli'.

My plant choices

This is a dramatic selection of plants chosen to bring diversity and interest to a relatively small area. If you want to expand this scheme, use more of the medium-sized (1m tall) plants to create swaying fields of colour punctuated with tall 'dot' plants throughout. Don't stint on bulbs – although not traditional prairie plants, they'll add much-needed colour before the perennials and grasses come to life in summer. My bulb choices also self-sow.

Bulbs

Plant as many as you can manage.

Allium caeruleum (AGM)

Flowers: JULY
Height/spread: 50CM
This fabulous member of the onion family has small, blue spherical flowers. New flowers sprout from the old, so spheres sit one on top of the other like multiple explosions. Plant bulbs in a sunny spot 5cm apart and 3cm deep as edgers. This allium self-seeds and provides interest before grasses start to flower.

Nectaroscordum siculum
Flowers: MAY–JUNE
Height/spread: 70CM X 10CM
Although no longer an allium, it's a close relative reclassified by botanists. Its large bells are subtly shaded pink and cream, and stand out well on tall elegant stems. It's a good self-seeder that's a favourite with bees.

Perennials
Plant in large swathes with a minimum of five plants per swathe.

Aster 'Little Carlow'
(*cordifolius hybrid*) (AGM)

Flowers: AUGUST–OCTOBER
Height/spread: 1M X 60CM
This late-flowering perennial forms a dome of small, lilac daisies. Its colour contrasts with the tawny tones of grasses and glows in low autumn sun. It's more resistant to powdery mildew than some asters, and is

tolerant of a little shade if you stake it well. Trim shoots by a third in May to make the stems shorter and more floriferous.

Echinacea purpurea 'Rubinstern' (AGM)

Flowers: AUGUST–OCTOBER
Height/spread: 90CM X 45CM
The ancestors of this upright perennial grow wild in prairies and on gravelly hillsides. Their solitary, daisy-like flowers are shaped like shuttlecocks surrounded by delicate, pink florets. Plant deep in well-drained, humus-rich soil in full sun and cut back the stems as the blooms fade to encourage more. Buy from a reputable nursery in spring (not in flower) and plant in situ to allow plants time to establish before flowering. They'll have a better chance of surviving winter this way. If you do buy in late summer, forgo the flowers in the first year, pruning them off with secateurs – this takes willpower but encourages the growth of stocky, well-rooted plants that flower all the better in subsequent years.

Echinops ritro 'Veitch's Blue'
Flowers: AUGUST
Height/spread: 90CM X 45CM
This plant has compact, spherical flowers of shimmering steely blue. Plants are fully hardy and grow best in poor but well-drained soil. They're tolerant and undemanding, and, because they readily self-seed, make a good partner for *Helianthus* 'Lemon Queen' (AGM) filling big borders fast.

Eupatorium purpureum

Flowers: AUGUST–SEPTEMBER
Height/spread: 2.2M X 1M
A tall, statuesque perennial that forms clouds of antique pink, plum or creamy white flowerheads. It's very effective when grown in big groups or as a flowering summer screen and bees, butterflies and hoverflies love it. It will take part-day shade and is easy from seed. Sow seed in containers in loam-based potting compost in a cold frame in spring, pot up individually, water freely and feed through the summer. By autumn you'll have plants big enough to go in the ground.

145

Helianthus 'Lemon Queen' (AGM)

Flowers: AUGUST–SEPTEMBER
Height/spread: 1.8M X 1M
With dainty yellow flowers rising above a cloud of veined, dark green leaves, this perennial is quite unlike the annual sunflowers we grow from seed. Plant in moist, well-drained soil in a sunny position but, be warned, it's a real spreader and needs to be kept in check. You can lift and divide it every year to colonise new areas or give clumps to friends. Clear back some roots in spring to keep them from smothering neighbouring plants.

Helenium
'Sahin's Early Flowerer' (AGM)
Flowers: JUNE–OCTOBER
Height/spread: 1.3M X 50CM
This good-looking, clump-forming perennial has daisy-like flowerheads with prominent yellowy-brown and orange florets. This variety has an incredibly long flowering period and is well suited to a sunny spot, in moist but well-drained soil in full sun. Provide support and deadhead to prolong flowering.

> 'Rising above a cloud of veined, dark-green leaves, *Helianthus* 'Lemon Queen' is quite unlike the annual sunflowers we grow from seed'

Persicaria amplexicaulis 'Firedance'
Flowers: JULY–NOVEMBER
Height/spread: 60CM X 60CM
This plant's dainty, bottle-brush blooms are held aloft on tall stems and make an excellent edging for a prairie as they mingle well with stiffer, more formal neighbours and create a natural look. When planted in groups the flowers form a froth of vivid salmon-red (and 'Rosea' is antique pink) that float over leafy, green foliage. This is an attractive, hardworking yet undemanding plant that grows quickly. It's best in moist soil in full sun but copes well on sandy/free-draining ground if given a little shade.

Rudbeckia fulgida var. *deamii* (AGM)
Flowers: AUGUST–OCTOBER
Height/spread: 60CM X 45CM
Cheerful yellow daisies grow on tall stems that give them a statuesque appearance. It grows wild in the moist meadows and light woodlands of North America – perfectly prairie. The yellow flowers have dark, conical centres and grow best in moderately fertile, well-drained soil. This particular cultivar is more drought-tolerant than other varieties.

Aster 'Little Carlow' forms a blue sea behind the blush-pink wands of *Persicaria rosea*.

Sedum (Herbstfreude Group)
'Herbstfreude' (AGM)
Flowers: AUGUST–SEPTEMBER
Height/spread: 60CM X 60CM

A classic, clump-forming perennial that puts on a show of star-shaped flowers that are deep pink turning to pinkish-bronze and copper-red. Grow in ordinary to moderately fertile, well-drained soil in a sunny, open spot. Divide every few years to keep plants stocky and reduce their need for staking.

Sedum 'Red Cauli' (AGM)
Flowers: SEPTEMBER–OCTOBER
Height/spread: 30CM X 30CM

Joe Swift introduced me to 'Red Cauli', with its tightly packed cauliflower-like blooms. It forms a mound of grey-green leaves that become flushed with purple tones as the weeks progress. In late summer small clusters of pale pink buds open to reveal bright pink flowers that age to red. It also produces eye-catching, deep maroon seedheads, extending its season into autumn. Grow as above.

Short Grasses
Use in drifts, at the front of borders and to edge paths.

Bouteloua gracilis
Flowers: AUGUST
Height/spread: 60CM X 30CM

This ornamental grass forms dense clumps of nodding, brown-green leaves and bears arching brown-purple flower panicles. It's useful for fresh or dried flower arrangements and great along path edges or in containers. It prefers slightly acid, sandy soils with a bit of protection in wet, cold winters.

Miscanthus sinensis 'Yakushima Dwarf'
Flowers: AUGUST–SEPTEMBER
Height/spread: 60CM X 50CM

An ideal grass for low-growing areas of prairie planting. Clumps form short, stout tufts of foliage that is green with white midribs. Small, pink and fluffy flowerheads emerge from the centre of the clump and turn silver with age. Don't cut this plant back until spring as it provides structure and interest through winter. Divide every few years to keep plants stocky and reduce their need for staking.

Panicum virgatum 'Heavy Metal'
Flowers: AUGUST ONWARDS
Height/spread: 1M X 70CM

A major component of the North American landscape, *Panicum virgatum* features heavily in many fine prairie-style borders. It's a deciduous plant that's stiff and upright in habit, with metallic blue-grey leaves that turn yellow in autumn. It's topped with masses of tiny purplish flowers, creating an attractive haze that moves with the slightest breeze. Grow in moist but well-drained soil in a sunny position.

Pennisetum alopecuroides 'Hameln'
Flowers: JULY–SEPTEMBER
Height/spread: 1M X 60CM

This deciduous grass is compact and early flowering. It has greenish-white flowers that turn grey-brown as they mature, and dark green leaves that turn golden-yellow in autumn. Ideal for small gardens and the front of borders. Its fuzzy, catkin-like flowers can be used fresh or dried in flower arrangements. Plant in a sunny spot in light, moderately fertile and well-drained soil.

Calamagrostis 'Karl Foerster' grasses stand sentinel amongst *eupatorium* and *asters* in autumn.

Tall grasses

Use to add height and punctuation amongst flower drifts. Plant singly or in groups of three.

Miscanthus sinensis 'Abundance'
Flowers: AUGUST–SEPTEMBER
Height/spread: 1.6M X 1.2M

An outstanding deciduous grass that forms compact mounds of attractive narrow leaves covered in masses of delicate buff-white flowers. It's perennial and, in my opinion, one of the very best miscanthus for general garden use – its flowers glint in the sunlight and hold all through the winter. Plant in fertile and moist but well-drained soil in full sun or light shade.

Miscanthus sinensis 'Gracillimus'
Flowers: AUGUST–SEPTEMBER
Height/spread: 1.3M X 1.2M

A long-established deciduous cultivar, grown for its fine-textured foliage that bleaches to a pale straw colour as winter sets in. It enjoys the same growing conditions as 'Abundance', although protect it from too much winter wet.

Calamagrostis x *acutiflora*
'Karl Foerster'
Flowers: JULY ONWARDS
Height/spread: 1.8M X 60CM

An upright bestseller of a grass which is easy to grow and is tolerant of most soil conditions, although it will reach its full potential in soil that's kept moist in summer. 'Karl Foerster' produces tall sheaves that start off pale green, turn to pink-bronze and eventually bleach to a straw colour late in the season. These fronds move in the breeze and last into the winter months. It's deciduous and fully hardy.

Your maintenance regime

Prairie borders look after themselves for large chunks of the year, although there are a few key tasks you'll need to keep on top of.

Spring

- In early spring cut back deciduous grasses including miscanthus, calamagrostis, panicum and pennisetum to within 15cm of their bases. Do this before signs of new spring growth.
- Weed between the crowns of plants and mulch with compost. Look out for weed grasses that self-sow amongst the crowns of their still-brown ornamental cousins.
- Divide perennials that have bare centres to their crowns and large grasses that flower late in summer (see page 151) just as they start to grow as this makes them less prone to rot.
- Take basal cuttings from perennial flowers to boost your stock and create plants for free (see page 153).
- Watch out for slugs and snails on new perennial growth, particularly in wet weather.

Summer

- Deadhead echinops, helenium and echinacea to prolong their flowering period long into autumn.
- Remove the top 10cm of sedums to encourage them to grow into stocky plants. The cuttings root easily, for new plants for free.
- Cut back *helianthus, asters and helenium* in May or June by 20cm. This increases the number of flowers, makes them more stocky and less likely to flop in wet weather.

Echinacea is loved by butterflies and bees.

Sheaves of 'Karl Foerster' create exclamation marks among a scrum of *helianthus, eupatorium* and *asters*.

Autumn
- Look out for and transplant any perennials that are being crushed by their neighbours.
- Use large labels to mark plants that have outgrown their space or need moving – they'll be a useful reminder come spring.
- Plant large drifts of bulbs in clusters amongst late perennials.
- Track down self-sown seedlings, dig them up and grow them on in a cold frame through winter. Plant out in spring where you want them to flower.
- If planting heleniums and Echinacea in late summer, when they're commonly available in garden centres, remove the flowers in their first year to encourage stronger-rooted, bushier plants.
- Collect ripe seed of grasses for sowing when it's plump and dry.

Winter
- Protect pennisetum roots from heavy frost with a winter mulch of composted bark.
- Take root cuttings from echinacea (see page 57).
- Cut down flowers and seedheads that have been ruined by winter weather.

Echinacea 'Arts Pride' has delicate flowers.

Techniques for the Modern Prairie

There are various techniques to increase the display of late-season perennials and grasses, including early-summer pruning for more flowers and propagation.

Summer cutbacks

Pinching out tall plants, such as asters and helenium, can help to make them bushier and self-supporting. The bushier a plant is, the more flowering stems and the more colourful your garden.

In June, using a sharp pair of secateurs, cut back stems by 10–20cm – the more you cut the more flowers you will get, though the later they will appear. This technique works by encouraging each stem to branch out, producing more flowering stems from below the cut, making it appear bushier and less leggy. It tends to delay the plant's natural flowering time, though, so you do take the risk that if autumn arrives early you won't have as long a display.

Taking basal cuttings

Take basal cuttings in the spring when stems are 5–10cm tall. It's a perfect technique for propagating many plants, including sedum, asters, echinacea, helenium and rudbeckia. It's a great technique for bulking up plants for planting the same growing season.

1: Hold the plant stem between finger and thumb and wiggle it in small circles until it breaks away from the crown.

2: If it has roots attached, pot up. If not, trim damaged ends with a sharp knife below a node and then pot up.

3: Pot a few stems into 12cm containers and grow on in a shaded cold frame, cold greenhouse or, for fast results, in a heated propagator. The stems will quickly root and grow away, and some will be ready to plant out in summer for flowering.

1

2

3

How to propagate grasses

A prairie border needs grasses, and lots of them, to create a soft swaying backdrop for more colourful flowers. Apart from splashing cash there are two ways to bulk up numbers quickly: by division and by sowing seed.

Sowing seed

You can buy ornamental grass seed or, even better, gather your own when it ripens in late summer. Not all collected seed will grow true, but it's still worth collecting and sowing, especially if you have lots of space to fill.

Sow seed any time between spring and autumn, scattering it evenly across a tray of compost. Cover the seed thinly with another dusting of compost. Water thoroughly with a fine rose and place in a propagator or cold frame (see below) for a fortnight – most seeds should germinate in this time. If they don't germinate, wrap the pots in freezer bags, put them in the fridge for a few weeks and try again. This should fool the seeds that winter has passed and break their dormancy. Grow the plants on until they are 5–10cm high and then plant small clumps (not individual seedlings) into 12cm pots. Keep the plants in a cold frame over winter before planting outdoors in spring.

Plants to germinate in a cold frame or cold greenhouse (15–18°C)

Anemanthele lessoniana (AGM)
Flowers: June–September
Height/spread: 1M X 1M
This handsome grass has bronze-tinged foliage and airy cascades of flowers in late summer. It works well planted in drifts or in a tall container. It's a good evergreen presence and is brilliant with spring bulbs.

Stipa tenuissima
Flowers: June–September
Height/spread: 60CM X 30CM
A native of dry, rocky slopes and exposed grasslands in New Mexico and Texas; it starts the year bright green fading to blonde through summer. Great for poor soils and sunny spots.

Plants to germinate in a propagator (20–25°C).

Bouteloua gracilis
See page 148 in the 'short grasses' section.

Miscanthus sinensis and hybrids
See page 149 in the 'tall grasses' section.

Pennisetum villosum (AGM)
Flowers: June–September
Height/spread: 50CM X 50CM
A spectacular grass with grey-green leaves and fluffy, white flowerheads in summer. It dies back over winter and should be given the protection of a warm wall in cold gardens.

How to propagate by division

Division is a sure way of getting a carbon copy of a parent plant (unlike sowing collected seed, which doesn't always come true), and grasses are ideal candidates. They're best divided in spring, just as they start to grow, when damage to roots quickly repairs, keeping rot at bay. That said, plants bought and divided in autumn work well if kept in a cold frame to recover. Divide grasses when clumps are at least 25cm across, following these simple steps.

Remove the whole plant from the ground with as many of its roots intact as possible (1). Tear the rootball apart, using two back-to-back forks as levers if the roots are tough (2). Replant large clumps, snipping off any parts that are dead and showing no sign of growth. Perk up the soil with fresh compost or soil improver and water well. You can keep dividing to make lots of plants, but the smaller the divisions the slower they'll be to catch up. My rule of thumb is to pot up and grow roots less than 9cm across in a cold frame rather than risk them in the ground, where they're likely to be smothered by larger neighbours.

1

Dividing new grasses

If you have patience and space, it's easy to create several new plants from a single grass bought from a nursery or garden centre. Do this in spring and use your fingers to tear the roots apart (tearing is better than cutting as less root is damaged). Some roots are as tough as nylon sacks. If this is the case, use a knife to get you started and finish by tearing. The number of new plants you create will depend on how large the original plant is, but you should be aiming for pieces of root that are at least 2cm across. Once divided, snip back the tops to 15cm and pot into 12cm containers. Water well and keep in a shady cold frame while they get over the shock, and as soon as they start to grow, give them sun. They'll be ready for replanting the following summer.

2

155

Erigeron blooms from
March to November.

8 | THE COASTAL GARDEN

The various borders and gardens at Greenacre have largely been created by improving soil to suit plants, but in the Coastal Garden the soil is poor, dry and sandy – so sandy in some places you could be at the beach, and we haven't improved it at all. If anything we've enhanced the drainage to allow us to grow a wider range of plants. Although it's far away from the coast, the plant selection is ideal for a salty seaside garden as well as land-locked gardens with dry soil.

The garden is about 5 metres wide and 8 metres long, and shaped like a wedge of cheese. In summer the ground is bone-dry and bereft of nutrients, as rain washes them away – quite like the soil you inherit if you've had a lot of building work done or if you buy a house on a new-build site. Luckily all is not lost and there are plenty of plants that love these conditions.

As my inspiration I took two sites that deal with dry soil particularly well – the Beth Chatto Gardens near Colchester, Essex, and the late Derek Jarman's plot at Dungeness. Both match plants to conditions they naturally thrive in. It's an environmentally friendly way to garden because plants are likely to be self-sufficient and healthy, needing less maintenance, watering and feeding to keep them alive.

This ecological style of gardening is now mainstream and has influenced how the majority of gardeners deal with really problematic places. If you're not sure whether your soil will suit these plants, the clues are a sandy, gritty texture making it difficult to dig, soil is shallow – less than 15cm deep – and plants wilt in summer and foliage yellows from lack of nutrients.

In a nutshell: *this is a modern version of a rock garden, with large plants that look good when they move in a breeze. Many have coastal origins, too, so are suitable for a seaside situation*

Suited to: *this style's for you if you've got a hot, dry garden with thin soil that's lacking in nutrients, or an exposed site*

Ideal location: *a sun-baked location is best*

Space needed: *you need a minimum of two square metres*

Maintenance rating: *low. If you use a weed-suppressing membrane this scheme will need very little looking after*

Eco credentials: *good. Many of the plants are attractive to bees and butterflies, and some produce seedheads that birds love*

1: *Euphorbia myrsinites*
2: *Lampranthus*
3: *Stipa tenuissima*
4: *Verbascum bombyciferum*
5: *Phormium* 'Sundowner'
6: *Elymus hispidus*
7: *Santolina chamaecyparissus*
8: *Eryngium giganteum*
9: *Limonium platyphyllum*
10: Decorative gabions lined with bottles and pebbles, planted with *Centranthus ruber* 'Albus' *Armeria maritama* and *Erigeron karvinskianus*
11: *Erigeron karvinskianus*
12: *Crambe maritima*
13: *Glaucium flavum* f. *fulvum*
14: *Eryngium pandanifolium*

N

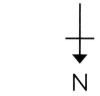

Coastal Garden elements

Pebbles

You can't have a coastal garden without pebbles, and I find they look best if you go for a mix of sizes. Five 25kg bags cover a square metre, although it is cheaper to buy tonne bags that cover eight or 10 square metres. Place the smallest pebbles directly onto weed-suppressing membrane, using shoals of larger pebbles on top for effect.

Weed-suppressing membrane

This excludes light and discourages weeds from germinating. Choose the soft, fabric type over woven nylon as it's easy and neat to cut then hide with pebbles. I only use membrane on unplanted areas (like paths), opting to mulch borders with pebbles alone – this makes it easier for plants to self-seed.

Timber uprights

Chunky timbers

These add height and character to borders. Look out for weathered, reclaimed timber posts at least 12cm thick in salvage and reclamation yards. The more gnarled and weather-worn they are the better. The oak timbers in Greenacre's coastal garden used to be steps. Avoid reclaimed railway sleepers, as they are now banned in the garden due to the carcinogenic, clothes-staining creosote they ooze in hot weather.

Gabions

Gabions are made from strong wire mesh and traditionally used to stabilise soil and prevent erosion on coastlines. They are simple to make and useful for low retaining walls as they need no foundations. They come flat-packed and are wired together in situ (see page 169). You can buy gabions online, although a local supplier made the ones at Greenacre. Our 30cm cubes cost £15 each, the 60cm cubes cost £25 each.

My plant choices

Coastal, drought-tolerant plants have evolved to survive where rainfall is sporadic or where the soil is dry and free-draining. Many have special ways of conserving water, like the hair-covered leaves of santolina designed to slow down moisture loss, while others stay low to the ground, shading the soil around their roots to stop moisture escaping. Some, like eryngium, have very deep, carrot-like roots to search for water, while others store moisture in their fleshy leaves.

Many coastal plants are prolific self-seeders, meaning they look after themselves once introduced. Self-sown plants acclimatise to the garden they find themselves in, growing large and lush if conditions allow or, if times are tough, staying small and compact, reproducing when young.

True coastal conditions also require plants to cope with salt-laden winds. There are many that do this, including shrubby, evergreen santolina, elymus and seathrift, crambe. In fact, a covering of salt crystals on crambe stops it dying out.

Evergreens
Use for permanent structure and winter interest, planting singly or in groups of three.

Euphorbia myrsinites (AGM)
Flowers: MAY ONWARDS
Height/spread: 15CM X 30CM
This is a ground-hugging plant, with succulent blue-green leaves and zesty, lime-green bracts. Remove spent flowers to keep plants neat and to show off emerging fresh leaves. Use this euphorbia as an edger so it gets the light it needs and to bring its evergreen leaves to the fore in winter.

Phormium 'Sundowner' (AGM)
Flowers: JULY
Height/spread: 2M X 2M
A lax-leaved evergreen with sheaves of arching foliage striped with coppery-red, pink and chocolate. Mature specimens grow to 2m tall and sometimes produce dramatic, zigzagging flower stems. Cut out tattered leaves in early spring along with any that have reverted in colour to green or grey-brown. It'll provide interest and stand out through winter. It's a good plant for exposed gardens on the coast and takes some shade.

Santolina chamaecyparissus (AGM)
Flowers: JULY
Height/spread: 50CM X 1M
Cotton lavender is a tough, knee-high, sprawling shrub with woolly, grey foliage. It has small, yellow pompom flowers, although you can trim these off if you'd rather just grow it for the leaves. Santolina thrives in dry weather, in fact the tougher the conditions the longer they live. They're also easy to propagate by taking summer cuttings (see 'Grow a lavender hedge from cuttings' page 71 for the best method). Trim plants in late summer to keep them in shape and stop them becoming bare at the base.

Cotton lavender thrives in hot sun and dry conditions.

Grasses

Grasses are perfect for a coastal garden as they can cope with strong winds and look wonderful swaying in a breeze.

Stipa tenuissima

Flowers: JUNE–SEPTEMBER
Height/spread: 60CM X 30CM

A small grass, which looks particularly good in swishing drifts around boulders. Comb out dead growth with your fingers in early spring, and replace plants when they start to look tired. It's a reliable self-seeder that looks beautiful back-lit by sunshine.

Elymus hispidus

Flowers: JULY (although they're not much to look at)
Height/spread: 75CM X 50CM

A knee-high grass which brings an authentic sand-dune look to a scheme. It's amazingly resilient to hot conditions thanks to its fleshy roots and silver leaves. Cut out the flowers to keep the plant tidy. It's short-lived so collect seed and re-sow every few years. It may also self-seed and spread of its own accord. Plant singly or in ribbons.

Perennials

Use perennials to inject colour and provide highlights of interest throughout the year.

Armeria maritima

Flowers: MAY–AUGUST
Height/spread: 20CM X 30CM

Thrift is a coastal-garden classic, which pops all around the British shoreline. I like the powder-pink drumsticks best, although white and dark pink forms are available. It will grow in extremely sandy soil as it has deep roots that hunt out moisture, and it self-seeds freely.

Centranthus ruber 'Albus'

Flowers: MAY–OCTOBER
Height/spread: 80CM X 45CM

A white form of valerian with textured, grey leaves and lovely airy flowers that give two flushes per year – one in late spring and another in late summer. It has really fleshy roots so is a survivor in inhospitable spots. It's also a magnet for bees and butterflies. Valerian self-seeds readily and profusely, so be careful it doesn't take over. If you start to feel overrun, deadhead plants as soon as they finish flowering – you'll miss out on fluffy seedheads, although it will encourage another flush of flowers. The dark red and pale pink forms are also excellent dry, garden plants.

Crambe maritima (AGM)

Flowers: JUNE
Height/spread: 60CM X 60CM
Sea kale has a mound of gun-metal-grey leaves that combine beautifully with pebbles. It also has tall flower stalks, each holding a dome of sea-spray-like blooms. Young stems emerge purple and can be eaten if covered for a week to exclude light and make them tender (fishwives would traditionally pile up stones over the crowns). Stems have a salty, cabbage-like flavour and are best steamed and served with a knob of butter, like asparagus. Sunlight is the key to growing crambe well, so give it your most sun-baked spot. It also self-seeds.

Erigeron karvinskianus (AGM)

Flowers: JUNE–OCTOBER
Height/spread: 30CM X 1M
This plant has semi-evergreen leaves and white daisies that are kissed with pink. It flowers for an incredibly long time amongst pebbles, cracks and crevices. Plants eventually create low airy mats of foliage and flower, helping to knit schemes together and cover bare gaps. Cut back dead and tatty growth in spring.

Eryngium giganteum (AGM)

Flowers: JUNE–AUGUST
Height/spread: 90CM X 30CM

A must-grow perennial with beautiful, silver thistle flowers that develop a metallic sparkle in dry conditions. It's a delicate-looking plant, but it doesn't need staking and it's perfectly proportioned. It's also called 'Miss Willmott's Ghost' after a nineteenth-century lady gardener who was apparently known for sprinkling the seed when she went garden visiting. I'm thinking of trying that!

Eryngium pandanifolium (AGM)
Flowers: JULY
Height/spread: 2.4M X 45CM

Silver-grey leaves with tall, spiky flowers that stay intact through winter and look stunning back-lit by low sunshine. Although a real showstopper, this plant doesn't enjoy severe winters. With this in mind, it's worth taking root cuttings to ensure you've always got spare plants in the wings (see page 57).

Glaucium flavum f. fulvum
Flowers: JUNE–AUGUST
Height/spread: 60CM X 30CM

This is a horned poppy that produces tangerine flowers that shimmer like a silk skirt. The foliage is silver-grey. The seedpods have long, curved, raptor-like claws, which are responsible for the plant's common name. As autumn approaches the pods dry and crack open, spilling their precious progeny about.

Limonium platyphyllum
Flowers: JULY–SEPTEMBER
Height/spread: 60CM X 45CM

Sea lavender creates an authentic coastal feel, as in the wild it colonises sand dunes, salt marshes and cliffs, particularly in the South West. It grows best in very free-draining soil and is loved by bees and butterflies. The papery lavender-blue flowers are borne on stiff, upright stems and are good for drying. Pinch out the first flowers for a bushy, floriferous plant.

Verbascum bombyciferum
Flowers: JULY–AUGUST
Height/spread: 1.8M X 60CM

This biennial verbascum starts life as a rosette of flat felt leaves, and shoots out tall flower spikes bearing tactile, wool-covered buds that open into small yellow blooms. It grows best in chalky soil, so is good amongst limestone chippings, but it does well at Greenacre. Leave spent flower spikes in place as they'll look good through winter and help the plant self-seed. Sow bought seed in spring at 15–18 °C and plant out in early summer.

Woolly flower spikes of *verbascum* soar to above head height.

Your maintenance regime

Think of a coastal garden as a low-maintenance herbaceous border – it'll benefit from deadheading but won't need as much time-consuming weeding and staking.

Spring
- Lift and weed out plants that have spread beyond their bounds – you're aiming for a good balance of order and self-sown abandon.
- Introduce new plants if you've got gaps or something isn't working. Water plants first, then trowel moisture-retaining garden compost into the hole before planting and watering them in.
- Trim dead leaves and flowerheads from evergreens and perennials.
- Shear back santolina to just above old growth to retain its bounce.

Summer
- Plant frost tender lampranthus-like bedding for a splash of summer colour. Plants will naturalise in mild locations but can be kept going year to year from cuttings.
- Water new plants in their first summer once a week in extremely dry weather.
- Take summer cuttings to ensure future generations of short-lived or slightly tender plants, such as lampranthus and santolina (see page 73).

Autumn
- Collect seeds of poppies, stipa and eryngium and sow to colonise bare areas.
- Take root cuttings of eryngium (see page 57).
- Remove spent foliage before it becomes soggy and decomposed amongst the pebbles.

Winter
- Sow seed of bought sea holly directly amongst the pebbles. Frosty winter weather will break its dormancy, so new plants sprout in the spring.
- Sow seed of sea lavender indoors in late winter, lightly covering it with vermiculite, and plant out after the first frosts of spring. Pinch out the first flowers for a bushy, floriferous plant.

Lampranthus ready for planting out after the frosts.

Techniques for the Coastal Garden

Taking summer stem cuttings is easy – simply snip off healthy stems roughly 10cm long, trim the base below a bud and then remove the leaves from the lower half of the cutting. Push into 10cm pots filled with moist multi-purpose compost. Keep the cuttings in a shady cold frame and they should root within a few weeks and be big enough to plant out the following spring. This propagation technique works with many coastal garden plants, including lampranthus, cotton lavender and *Euphorbia myrsinites* (AGM).

Weeding amongst pebbles can be tricky. Pull tap-rooted weeds like dandelions from amongst pebbles. If you've got sandy soil, do this directly after rain and, with luck, they'll come out of the soil roots and all. If they don't come out in one piece, temporarily remove pebbles from around the offending plant and dig it out.

Midden piles

Creating a midden pile is a clever way of getting plants to grow in inclement or dry spots. Whilst filming *Gardeners' World* at Dungeness I met a gardener and contemporary artist called Paddy Hamilton. He gardens a dry-shingle plot in Kent and taught me the technique. It's very simple.

Place piles of ripe seedheads with the stalks attached where nothing will grow and leave them alone. The seeds will often germinate under the shelter of their own decaying stem litter, which protects them from dry winds and keeps them moist while they sprout.

The technique also works with bought seeds – sprinkle them over the ground in autumn (herbaceous perennials) or early spring (annuals) and then place herbaceous prunings over the top. You can continue to add seeds as you collect them, simply scattering the seeds into the pile.

Check regularly for sprouting and remove the prunings when you see signs of growth.

Introducing permanent structure

Timbers and gabions add height and character to the Coastal Garden at Greenacre. They also provide structure to plant around. Here's how to make them work in your garden.

How to use timbers

Pieces of chunky timber echo the groynes at the beach and anchor soft landscaping. Find suitable positions for your uprights by initially substituting them for bamboo canes. This way you can easily play around with different heights and locations, without the need to lug great pieces of wood about. Regularly stand back to check the arrangement looks good from all angles, especially the main views from the house.

Timbers need fixing in the soil with concrete to ensure they stay upright and aligned and don't topple over. The taller the timber the deeper the hole needs to be.

Dig out 15cm for posts up to 80cm tall and 30cm for posts up to 1.5m tall. To ensure they are firmly anchored, add a 30cm length of metal thread-rod (buy this from DIY stores) to the base of the timbers (drill a 12cm-deep hole in the bottom and push the rod in) before placing them in the ground. Drive the rod into the soil at the bottom of the hole, make sure the post is level and add ready-mixed, fast-setting concrete (the type used for fence posts is ideal) to just below the level of the surrounding soil. Add water and use a trowel to slope the sides of the concrete away from the wood to prevent water collecting at the base of the wood and rotting it.

Improve the soil around the base of each timber with compost before planting, then hide the base of the timber with large pebbles. Vary the height of the timbers for the best effect.

How to make gabion planters

Gabions are galvanised wire boxes filled with stones, traditionally used in civil-engineering projects to retain soil and reinforce sea defences. However, they also make interesting garden planters, and can be used to create low walls and seats and require little-to-no construction skills to make.

All gabions come flat-packed so the first job is to wire them together. Some systems use clips, while others use wire spirals. Use pliers to bend any sharp ends of wire back on themselves, and then position gabions in their final spot before filling them. Also check they are level. If you're making a seat or wall, wire several gabions together before filling them. The gabions at Greenacre consist of one wire box inside another. The small box in the middle holds soil like a container and needs to be lined with weed-suppressing membrane to stop the soil falling out (1). The outside box can be filled with a façade of pebbles, chain, collected driftwood and bottles (2). Place bottles upside-down to prevent water collecting and beetles and voles getting trapped inside. Plant up with thrift and valerian (3), and cover the soil with pebbles and small pieces of driftwood (4). Give plants a drink, and remember to water in dry weather.

1

2

4

3

Poppies, *godetia*, *phacelia* and cornflowers jostle with white *ammi umbels*.

9 | THE SEED-PACKET MEADOWS

Unlike a true meadow of native wildflowers, the meadow at Greenacre is made up of a colourful mix of hardy annuals sourced from seed catalogues. It's an easy and eye-popping way to bring bare soil to life, creating large seas of summer colour at relatively little cost. You can either create your own seed mix or buy ready-made blends of flowers known as 'pictorial' meadows, created to be different heights or colours, or suited to a particular location.

One of the main reasons we sow an annual meadow at Greenacre is to look after the soil, and to make sure areas aren't left bare for long periods of time. Bare soil is at severe risk, as rain washes its nutrients away and separates soil particles into bands of different sizes. This is particularly apparent with Greenacre's sandy clay-loam, which forms a biscuit-hard, impenetrable layer after lots of rain. Over time another layer develops 40cm below the surface where clay and iron particles lock together to form a solid pan. This damage to soil structure, and the loss of fertility, is extremely time-consuming to put right, and covering the ground with annual flowers has been key in keeping our earth in good shape. It's also a handy way to keep weeds at bay.

Seed-packet meadows, like the wildflower versions that inspire them, are at their best when re-sown with new mixes over a number of years. By doing this a meadow is enriched in the most surprising ways from summer to summer, as seeds that have fallen and lain dormant from previous sowings wake and flower. Often they'll miss a year and then reappear like mementoes from summers past.

In a nutshell: *this is a colourful mix of hardy annuals that have the look of a native meadow but don't need as much maintenance*

Suited to: *sow an annual meadow if you have lots of space to fill or virgin borders. Or if you just want a meadow look and don't mind a bare border in winter*

Ideal location: *open ground in a sunny site*

Space needed: *you need a minimum of two square metres, although the larger the area the more impressive it will look*

Maintenance rating: *moderate. You'll need to spend time sowing seed in the spring, followed by regular weeding throughout the growing season*

Eco credentials: *excellent. If you choose the right seed mix a meadow like this will attract a range of bees, butterflies and birds*

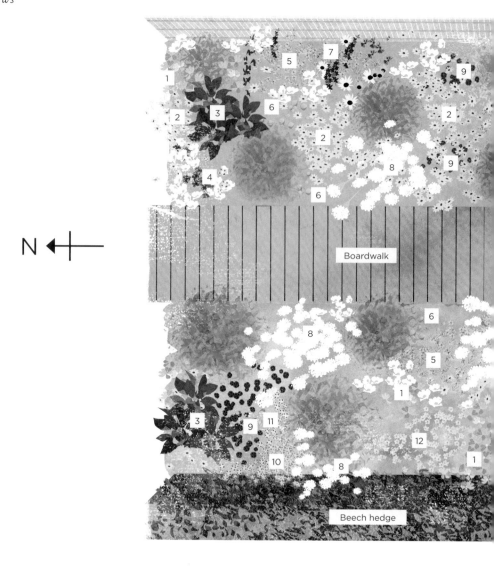

Annual meadow elements

Flowers

Use hardy annuals for your meadow. They have flowers that live and die in a season, and seed that germinates when sown direct into soil in spring.

Location

Choose an open, sunny site or slugs will be more of a problem. Your meadow doesn't need to be in the same place every year, as you can re-sow it where you like every spring. Alternatively, re-sow in the same place and allow last year's relics to add to the mix. I love the colourful and chaotic effect this creates.

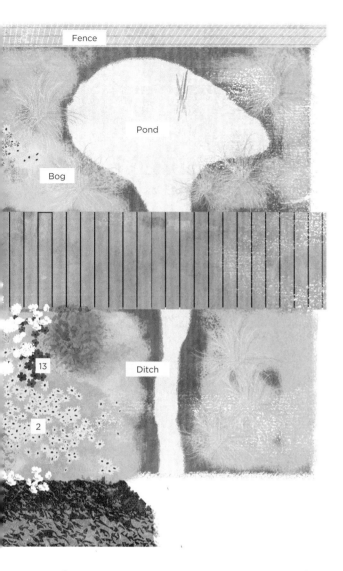

1: *Cosmos bipinnatus*
2: *Coreopsis tinctoria*
3: *Atriplex hortensis*
4: *Linum grandiflorum 'Rubrum'*
5: *Phacelia tanacetifolia*
6: *Eachscholzia californica*
7: *Consolida ajacis*
8: *Ammi majus*
9: *Papaver commutatum*
10: *Centaurea cyanus*
11: *Clarkia amoena*
12: *Nigella damascena*
13: *Papaver rhoeas*

Wildlife

Choose your mix to benefit wildlife. For example, a meadow of sunflowers will be a boon for seed-eating birds, while phacelia is a boon for numerous insects including bees, hoverflies and lacewing. Simple flowers with plenty of nectar and pollen are perfect for bees, so make sure you include cornflowers, nigella, poppies and larkspurs in the mix.

Mono-meadow

One of the meadows at Greenacre is pretty much all cosmos with a little larkspur and millet to attract birds. It covers a huge area, flowers from June until November and its simplicity is extremely effective. Don't feel you have to include lots of different flowers if you like simple schemes.

My plant choices

Seed packet mixes can have fifty or more species and varieties, which is far too many to include here. As a result, this is my selection of the annuals that have really earned their space at Greenacre.

Ammi majus

Flowers: JUNE–SEPTEMBER
Height/spread: 1.2M X 50CM

With its large, dainty white umbels, this plant looks a little like a cowslip with fern-like green leaves. It creates billowing clouds of ethereal white flowers when planted in swathes, and is a florists' favourite, adding a romantic froth to formal bouquets.

Atriplex hortensis var. rubra

Flowers: JULY–AUGUST
Height/spread: 150CM X 30CM

If *Ammi majus* is dainty, then this red orache is a plant with bulk. It's mostly grown for its spinach-like, edible purple leaves that are good in salads, although its colourful foliage works really well in a meadow, too. Plants become enthusiastic self-seeders, and it always bolts, so just collect the seed and chop it down if you're worried about it spreading to borders where it shouldn't be.

Centaurea cyanus

Flowers: JUNE–AUGUST
Height/spread: 90CM X 30CM

The pretty blue cornflower is a cottage-garden favourite, easy to grow and looks very much at home in a meadow. The flowers are edible and add a flash of unexpected colour to salads. The good thing about growing cornflowers 'meadow-style' is that the wiry stems are supported amongst the mesh of plants.

Clarkia amoena

syn. Godetia Azalea-Flowered Mixed
Flowers: JUNE–SEPTEMBER
Height/spread: 45CM X 30CM

A showy summer annual with cup-shaped flowers and paper-thin petals. It comes in virtually every shade of pink and is a member of the evening primrose family. This plant grows vigorously on erect, slender stems and, in the wild, thrives on open slopes. Over-fertile soil encourages foliage growth at the expense of flowers.

'Larkspur comes in rich tones or pastel shades of pink, lavender, carmine, white or violet, individual flowers are orchid-like and loved by bees'

Consolida ajacis

Flowers: JUNE–SEPTEMBER
Height/spread: 1M X 30CM

Resembling delphiniums in shape and structure, larkspur produces energetic spires of elegant flowers. Available in rich tones or pastel shades of pink, lavender, carmine, white or violet, individual flowers are orchid-like and loved by bees. Young plants are popular with slugs and snails, so be vigilant.

Coreopsis tinctoria

Flowers: JULY–SEPTEMBER
Height/spread: 60–90CM X 45CM

One of my favourite meadow plants, these cheerful summer daisies have bright yellow petals with a pretty maroon splodge in the centre. They make a vivid counterpoint for any sea of summer annuals, and are perfect for a meadow as they bloom for a long time without the need for deadheading. Their stiff stems are branching too, so you get plenty of daisies per plant. They're native to North America where they grow wild in abundance, mainly in areas with regular rainfall.

Cosmos bipinnatus

Flowers: JULY–SEPTEMBER
Height/spread: 70CM–1.5M X 45CM

I love cosmos. Available in shades of pink, purple and white, these tall, bushy annuals self-seed freely. Flowers are bowl- or saucer-shaped and appear throughout summer. The fine, thread-like foliage creates a supportive tangle for the top-heavy flowers, helping them float above the ground when grown in swathes. Deadheading prolongs flowering. For the longest flowering period, combine short cultivars like the 'Sonata Series' that only grow to 60cm and come into bloom earlier than the taller types.

Eschscholzia californica (AGM)
Flowers: JUNE–SEPTEMBER
Height/spread: 30CM X 15CM
The distinctive Californian poppy – see page 97 for details.

Linaria maroccana
Flowers: JUNE–SEPTEMBER
Height/spread: 70CM X 15CM
This pretty plant is also called 'Toadflax', which hardly seems fair. It hails from North Africa and is also known as a baby snapdragon, as its exotic-looking flowers have rounded velvety lips that resemble a small antirrhinum. It's available in vivid shades of violet, purple, pink, yellow, orange and white, and the bottom petals are sometimes marked with a contrasting flash of white, orange or yellow.

Linum grandiflorum 'Rubrum'
Flowers: JUNE–SEPTEMBER
Height/spread: 45CM X 15CM
The scarlet flax has crimson-red, saucer-shaped flowers with a dark bull's eye at their centre. The stems are erect, slender and downy. It works brilliantly in a meadow setting, blending despite its vivid colour.

Nigella damascena
Flowers: JULY–SEPTEMBER
Height/spread: 50CM X 20CM
Love-in-a-mist is a classy, pretty, easy-to-grow flower. Its pale blue flowers quiver above feathery foliage, with ruff-like surrounds and perky antenna-like stamens. After flowering, the heads turn into swollen green seed capsules, striped burgundy with a wispy fringe. It's a lovely flower for cutting.

Papaver commutatum (AGM)
Flowers: JUNE–AUGUST
Height/spread: 45CM X 15CM
This cultivated relative of our native corn poppy is similar in shape, but richer in colour and more robust-looking. Solitary bowl-shaped flowers are a shiny pillar-box red on stout, downy stems. Each petal bears a large black spot at its base. William Thompson (of Thompson & Morgan fame) developed the species from plants found in Russia in 1876, and they are as beautiful now as they were then.

Papaver rhoeas

Flowers: JUNE–AUGUST
Height/spread: 70CM X 30CM
With its saucer-shaped flowers and tissue-paper petals, the Shirley poppy is a cultivated variety of our iconic annual wildflower. From its furry buds and downy stems to its silky flowers and neat little seed capsules, these poppies delight right through the summer. Bred by the Reverend W. Wilks – vicar of Shirley in Surrey – more than a century ago, the Shirley poppy is available in all manner of flamboyant variants.

Delicate Shirley poppies and *linaria* flowering in high summer.

Your maintenance regime

Creating a seed-packet meadow is one of the fastest ways to make a big, floriferous impact – follow these guidelines for a sea of summer blooms.

Spring

- Prepare your site and sow seeds as described on page 183.
- Be vigilant for slug and snail damage, taking preventative measures at the first sign of attack (see page 181).
- Keep cats from scratching by popping some peasticks into the soil.

Mid-summer

- Make written notes of successes and failures throughout the growing season. This will help you make seed choices in subsequent years.
- Keep on top of weeds. Use sticks to gently fold back the meadow flowers and create a path for you to access offenders without crushing any blooms.
- Be vigilant for pests, particularly aphids, and spray with a mineral soap.

Late-summer and autumn

- Collect seed and store (see page 180) that of flowers you particularly like for sowing next year.
- Pull out flowers which have gone over if they spoil the look of later-flowering cosmos and coreopsis, for example.

Winter

- Compost spent annuals when they've been caught by frost and are looking messy.
- Dig out thistles, grasses and perennial weeds when the site is clear.
- Mulch the empty border to keep down weeds and protect the soil structure.

The view across the meadow when it was mostly cosmos in its first year.

Techniques for the Seed-Packet Meadows

The trick here is to balance copious numbers of plants, roguing out the self-sowers and propagating new plants as cheaply as possible.

Roguing

A rogue is a self-sown plant that doesn't fit your scheme. Pull out rogues that rise up in your meadow before they set seed. If they can't be reached from the outside of your meadow, create a temporary path for your feet by pushing back the stems of the flowers you want to keep with sticks.

Collecting and storing seed

It makes sense to collect as much seed as you can to save money on next year's meadow. I like to do it the old-fashioned way, with a method called winnowing. Here's how to do it.

1: Pick the pods and seedheads of flowers you like on a dry, sunny day in late summer. Pop them into individual A4 envelopes, label them and hang in a shed or greenhouse for a few weeks. I peg them like washing to a string line in my greenhouse roof.

2: Once everything is completely dry and crispy, you need to separate the seed from the chaff (seed casings, old petals, bits of stem and spent parts of the flowers). Start by scrunching the seedheads on a large piece of flexible card – I'm using an A4 envelope.

3: Gently toss the scrunched-up seedheads into the air while blowing across the top. The chaff, being lighter, blows away while the seed stays on the envelope. It helps if you bend the envelope a little so the seeds stays in place.

4: Place seeds in a jar on a 2cm layer of rice to keep them dry. Keep them cool and dry in a cupboard indoors.

2

3

1

How to sow an annual meadow

Seed-packet annuals come and go over the growing season, changing the appearance and colours of a meadow from week to week. Success is down to the sowing. I use a minimum of three packets of flower seed for every 10m square of meadow – assuming there are at least 100 seeds in each packet. For a richer mix, sow double the amount. Blend seed of short and tall varieties together for the longest display as the lower growers often bloom weeks before taller types get going. Or make the most of the height difference by grouping varieties of similar size together or using smaller flowers on their own around the edge. Then it's down to the weeding. Even on cleared ground weeds creep in, but you can still keep on top by roguing out offenders when they come up to flower (see page 18).

1: Clear your site of weeds in early spring, leave it to settle for a couple of weeks and rake it to a tilth to create a seedbed. Apply a slow-release, high-phosphate fertiliser to encourage plenty of flowers – bonemeal is ideal – and rake it into the surface of the soil. Get rid of clods and stones at the same time and tread flat. In poor, sandy or heavyday soil, add garden compost first to improve the structure.

I

2: Choose a fine, dry day to sow when soil is moist but not sodden. Mix your seed in a bucket, adding a few handfuls of dry sand to add bulk and help you to see where you're spreading seed for even coverage. I use a handful of sand for every metre of earth. Divide the mix into two. Broadcast one half over the complete area, and use the other half to fill in any missed spots or lightly covered areas. Rake the sand and seeds into the soil and wait. If the weather is very dry water the area, if not, sit back and wait for the ground to green up with seedlings and the place to come alive with colour.

Put out wildlife-friendly slug pellets and top up after rain. Keep cats and birds away with fruit-cage netting stretched over the beds supported on wire or bamboo hoops.

2

A pail of cosmos, poppies, *Dahlia* 'Rothesay Reveller' and squirrel-tail grass.

10 | THE CUT FLOWER GARDEN

Years ago I had a job as a gardener in America, tending the suburbs of Seattle. My route to work took me past a smallholding that sold cut flowers, and it's a place that's been stamped on my memory ever since. The plot itself wasn't huge, roughly the size of a tennis court, but it was such a floral mardi gras, with yellow 'Teddy Bear' sunflowers growing as a hedge, corralling blocks of zinnias and marigolds in every shade of cream, coral, sunshine-yellow and orange. What appealed to me then, and still does today, was the ethos of beauty through utility – even the functional things (colourful buckets, spools of twine, a wooden hand-cart with a primrose yellow parasol to keep the harvest cool) were lovely to look at.

Since I returned to England, I've always had a place of my own to gather armfuls of flowers, guilt-free without diminishing the rest of the garden – all inspired by the plot in Seattle. Lisa and I even dedicated a small patch of our front garden to growing flowers and petal confetti for our wedding.

Having enjoyed cut flowers at home for so many years, it was inevitable I would include a cut-flower patch at Greenacre. It's a rectangle of soil roughly 5 metres wide and 8 metres long, which lies in the lea of a beech hedge with a central brick path. This path is pretty and practical, allowing easy access and warming the soil along its edges so that flowers nearby come into bloom earlier than their neighbours. The Cut Flower Garden is a huge success, with everyone on the *Gardeners' World* team enjoying the blooms in the garden and then again in jars and vases in our offices.

In a nutshell: *this scheme offers flowers to cut from January to November*

Suited to: *anyone who loves fresh, seasonal cut flowers in their house*

Ideal location: *a discreet, sunny area of your garden or an allotment or veg patch*

Space needed: *you need a minimum of 4 square metres for five rows of flowers*

Maintenance rating: *high. Cut flowers need year-round care including sowing seed, weeding, deadheading and planting*

Eco credentials: *excellent. Lots of the flowers in a cutting garden are beneficial to bees, butterflies and birds*

1: *Acanthus mollis*
2: Chrysanthemums: 'Beppie Red', 'Energy' and 'Orange Allouise'
3: *Alchemilla mollis*
4: *Delphinium* 'Magic Fountains Dark Blue with White Bee'
5: *Leucanthemum vulgare* 'Maiknigin'
6: *Centaurea cyanus* 'Black Boy'
7: Pots of sweet peas: *Lathyrus odoratus* 'Albutt Blue' and *Lathyrus odoratus* Heirloom Bicolour Mixed
8: *Dahlia* 'Magenta Star'
9: *Lupinus* 'Gallery Yellow' and 'Gallery White'
10: *Dahlia* 'Rothesay Reveller'

Beech hedge

Cutting Garden elements

Cost

The name of the game is to concentrate on harvests that are economical to grow but expensive to buy. Summer annuals are just the ticket because they are cheap, quick to grow and offer huge variety. They're also really prolific and just the thing to use if you want to grow flowers for a summer wedding as Lisa and I did.

Experiment

A cut-flower patch offers a liberating chance to grow flowers that don't fit in other parts of your garden. Try unusual blooms, flowers that get overwhelmed when grown in company and even things that you might think too gaudy. Remember, what might be too brash for a border is almost certainly going to look good in a vase – when it comes to dahlias, for example, the bigger and more dramatic the better.

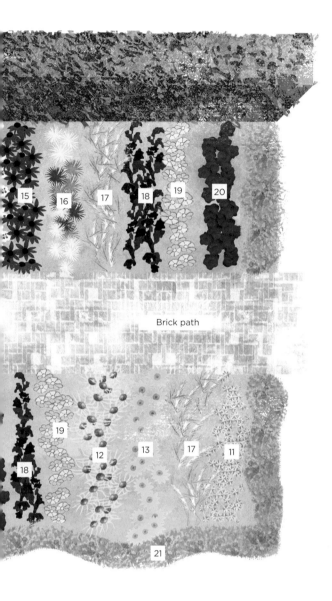

Brick path

11: *Nigella damascena* 'Persian Jewels Mix'

12: *Dipsacus fullonum*

13: *Helianthus annuus* 'Little Leo'

14: *Papaver somniferum* 'Hen and Chickens'

15: *Rudbeckia hirta* 'Cherry Brandy'

16: *Zinnia elegans* 'Giant Cactus-Flowered Mixed'

17: *Hordeum jubatum*

18: *Gladiolus*: 'Black Star' and 'atom'

19: *Cosmos bipinnatus* 'Candy Stripe'

20: *Antirrhinum majus* 'Black Prince'

21: Lavender hedge

N

Rows

To maximise yield, grow your flowers in organised rows, just as you would veg. This allows lots of flowers to be packed in, and makes weeding, tending and gathering easy. You'll also find it helps you to mix and match blooms – just pick a centrepiece and walk up and down the rows gathering others that go with it by the armful.

Premium range

A good cutting garden should include a collection of perennials – the spires of delphiniums, candy-coloured lupins and blousy chrysanthemums – that are magnificent, fleshy and seldom for sale in a florist, let alone on the high street. Compared to the quick-to-grow annuals they are expensive to buy, but they're easy to propagate from basal cuttings and division (see pages 151 and 153) and over time you get to gather them by the vase-full.

My plant choices

My plant selection includes a range of flowers grown from seed, bulbs and plugs. I've aimed for a long flowering period for picking from early spring right through to late autumn. To make life easy there are also some perennials, including foliage fillers.

Annuals and short-lived perennials
For quick returns at low cost from seed

Antirrhinum majus 'Black Prince'
Flowers: JUNE–SEPTEMBER
Height/spread: 45CM X 30CM

I love snapdragons and this variety has plump, deep-burgundy flowers, as soft and sumptuous as velvet, which attract bees like a magnet. It has dark green, bronze-tinted foliage and will continue flowering for as long as you deadhead spent blooms. Cut stems when about a third of the flowers are open and they'll last for ages indoors. Plants can survive mild winters.

Centaurea cyanus 'Black Boy'

Flowers: MAY–JULY
Height/spread: 1M X 15CM

This dramatic annual cornflower has shiny, dark-burgundy flowers with black inner florets. It's also perfect for cutting and easy to arrange in a vase. It's easily grown – keep cutting to keep it going for longer.

Cosmos bipinnatus 'Candy Stripe'
Flowers: JULY–SEPTEMBER
Height/spread: 90CM X 40CM

Both its feathery foliage and candy-striped flowers make this a cut-flower favourite. Don't feed or you'll get giant plants and no flowers. Deadhead to prolong blooms. Put them in a jug on the windowsill where their dainty petals will be lit from behind.

Dipsacus fullonum
Flowers: JULY–AUGUST
Height/spread: 1M X 50CM

Teasel is a prickly customer for cutting and arranging, but the flowers certainly add an architectural flourish to displays and the birds love the seedheads if you leave them standing in the garden into late autumn. They're hardy, biennial plants that produce a rosette of toothed, dark green leaves covered in spiny pustules, but these usually wither before the thistle-like, pinkish-purple or white flowers appear. Harvest the flowers and dry them – I spray them silver for home-spun Christmas decorations.

Helianthus annuus 'Little Leo'

Flowers: JULY–OCTOBER
Height/spread: 45CM X 30CM

Sunflowers are easy to grow and make a big splash in a vase. 'Little Leo' is a dwarf type with golden-yellow flowers. Sunflowers ideally need half a day's worth of direct sunlight and moist soil. They also need long hot summers to flower well.

Helianthus annuus 'Black Magic'

Flowers: JUNE–OCTOBER
Height/spread: 1.5M X 60CM

Here's an unusual, dramatic idea for those who shun cheerful yellow in the garden – black sunflowers. Okay, they're rich burgundy, but they're great for the back of border, as annual screening or, in this instance, as cut flowers. Sow the seed in fertile, moist but well-drained soil from March to May outdoors. They like full sun. Keep from spreading beyond rows by snipping off side-shoots. Birds love the seed.

'Squirrel-tail grass has arching, light green leaves and broad, silky panicles in a pale green flushed red or purple'

Hordeum jubatum

Flowers: JUNE–JULY
Height/spread: 50CM X 30CM

Squirrel tail-grass has arching, light green leaves and broad, silky panicles in a pale green flushed red or purple (they turn beige with age). It adds sparkle and texture when cut, vased and placed in sunshine. Grow in fertile, moist but well-drained soil in full sun. Cut the panicles off for drying before they reach full maturity. Use fresh with other flowers or when dry.

Heirloom sweet peas twining their way up a willow wigwam.

Lathyrus odoratus 'Albutt Blue'

Flowers: MAY–SEPTEMBER
Height/spread: 1.8M X 60CM

Sweetly scented, scrambling summer climber producing a constant supply of posies through summer. The picotee-edged flowers are duck-egg blue. Sow indoors in autumn for the earliest flowers in May, or March for blooms from June. Plant in compost-enriched soil in groups of three or five. Keep flowers coming by removing all spent blooms before they go to seed and keeping the roots watered in dry weather. 'Heirloom Bicolour Mixed' is worth growing for its good mix of pinks, plums, purples and whites and old-fashioned fragrance.

Moluccella laevis

Flowers: JUNE–SEPTEMBER
Height/spread: 75CM X 23CM

The intricate stems of pale-green Bells of Ireland make very versatile cut flowers. They're an interesting foil for deep-burgundy, black, red or white bouquets, but also making a dramatic modern statement all on their own. The small, tubular, hooded flowers are born in whorls, and are vaguely reminiscent of a cottage-garden foxglove with a sophisticated, modern twist. Grow in a moderately fertile, moist but well-drained soil in part or full sun. They're trouble-free and attract few pests.

Nigella damascena 'Persian Jewels Mix'

Flowers: JULY–SEPTEMBER

Height/spread: 50CM X 20CM

This collection of love-in-a-mist pop up in a range of colours, including sky-blue, violet-blue, rose-pink, deep pink and white. See page 176 for more details.

Papaver somniferum 'Hen and Chickens'

Flowers: JUNE–OCTOBER (with seedpods throughout this period)

Height/spread: 1.2M X 30CM

This poppy isn't grown for its flowers, which are rather short-lived, it's grown for its gigantic blue-green seedpods, which are surrounded by clusters of much smaller capsules, and is great for arrangements.

Rudbeckia hirta 'Cherry Brandy'

Flowers: JULY–OCTOBER

Height/spread: 60CM X 30CM

Widely hailed as the world's first red rudbeckia, this novelty award-winning (short-lived) perennial has a conical centre and daisy-like florets. It's a superb cut flower which blooms right the way through to the first frosts and looks great with squirrel-tail grass inside and out.

Zinnia elegans

'Giant Cactus-Flowered Mixed'

Flowers: JULY–SEPTEMBER

Height/spread: 90CM X 30CM

As colourful as a Mexican piñata and cheerful as a box of jumping beans, annual zinnias grow in a carnival of riotous abundance from midsummer onwards. Sow them in late spring, direct in situ, and let them get on with it. Their daisy-like flowers are borne on long stems that are perfect for cutting and displaying in vases.

Bulbs, tubers and corms

Plants for the wow factor.

Dahlia 'Rothesay Reveller'

Flowers: JUNE–OCTOBER

Height/spread: 1M X 70CM

All dahlias make statuesque cut flowers, but I picked this one for Greenacre for its raspberry ripple flowers that appear on long stems in abundance right through summer. Dahlias need well-drained soil and a sunny location. Only cut those with open flowers as buds seldom open once they're in a vase.

Gladiolus 'Black Star'

Flowers: JULY–SEPTEMBER

Height/spread: 1M X 20CM

'Black Star' is hard to miss. It has huge mahogany-red flowers, which are almost black and gorgeous in a vase. We plant the corms successively to keep the flowers coming throughout the season (it takes around 100 days from planting to flower). Stake to protect from strong winds. Pick when the bottom flowers are fully open.

Gladiolus nanus 'Atom'
Flowers: JUNE
Height/spread: 60CM X 20CM

Nanus hybrids flower in early summer and are ideal for cutting and using for corsages. This one is fiery orange, with a white splash around the edge of its petals – as though someone has been creative with a paintbrush. Corms produce two or three slender flower spikes whose stems are strong enough to render staking unnecessary.

Narcissus

There's no better way to put spring in your garden (or one in your step) than planting rows of daffs. The sight of them swaying in the early spring breeze is truly life-affirming. They look good planted in rows and in the vase. My favourites for picking include the January-flowering 'Rijnveldt's Early Sensation', 'Quail' for mid-spring followed by the fragrant poeticus type 'Geranium',

'There's no better way to put spring in your garden (or one in your step) than planting rows of daffs. The sight of them swaying in the eraly spring breeze is truly life-affirming'

which flowers with the tulips in May (see page 110–13 for more information).

Perennials

These are your bread and butter, providing cut flowers year after year.

Acanthus mollis
Flowers: MAY–AUGUST
Height/spread: 1.5M X 90CM

A vigorous, imposing perennial with tall flower spikes. Grow these as sentinels on bed corners (rather than in rows) as they need a bit of space to grow, and use gloves as the flowers have spikes. This plant will tolerate any soil in sun or a little shade, although it thrives in deep, fertile, well-drained loam.

Alchemilla mollis (AGM)
Flowers: JUNE–SEPTEMBER
Height/spread: 60CM X 75CM

This reliable little perennial is a useful addition to the Cut Flower garden. Its acid-green flowers make contrasting frothy foils for purple and orange flowers that are both long-lasting and robust. It's downy rounds of foliage catch perfect shiny beads of rain and dew. Delightful!

Asparagus officinalis
Height/spread: 1.5M X 90CM

I know what you're thinking: you can't grow asparagus shoots and put them in a vase – they're far too delicious swimming in hot butter with Sunday lunch. You're right, of course, but besides the tasty young spears this useful evergreen perennial also bears armfuls of decorative ferny, feathery foliage and tiny white bell flowers.

The stunning picotee petals of *Gladiolus* 'Atom'.

'Orange Allouise' is an old-fashioned cut flower for a retro feel.

Chrysanthemum 'Orange Allouise'
Flowers: SEPTEMBER–OCTOBER
Height/spread: 90CM X 40CM
An old variety, that's very reliable outdoors and weather resistant. The orange, ball-like flowers begin their show in September and last long into October. For the biggest blooms, grow three or four single stems, removing the other side-shoots as they develop. You can have more but the flowers will be smaller.

Chrysanthemum 'Beppie Red'
Flowers: SEPTEMBER–OCTOBER
Height/spread: 90CM X 40CM
A compact, good-natured garden 'mum' with a proven ability to grow outdoors. It's a spray variety, and for the best display leave five or six side-shoots per stem and pinch out the centre flower. If you don't do this it will open earlier than the rest and steal all the energy from the spray. Like all chrysanths it likes well-drained soil with compost around roots at planting time. It also does well from a fortnightly feed of tomato fertiliser when it runs up to flower. We also grew 'Primrose Enbee Wedding' in exactly the same way.

Chrysanthemum 'Energy'
Flowers: SEPTEMBER–OCTOBER
Height/spread: 90CM X 45CM
This dazzling quill-flowered chrysanthemum blooms in a dramatic shade of zingy lime green. To produce large flowers, remove all buds and side-shoots, just leaving the terminal (top) bud. To produce a spray, do the opposite, remove the terminal bud and leave all the side buds. Staking with peasticks is essential. For the biggest choice, order chrysanths from a specialist mail-order supplier who will dispatch plugs when they're ready to plant in spring.

Delphinium 'Magic Fountains Dark Blue with White Bee'
Flowers: MAY–JULY
Height/spread: 60CM X 40CM
Dwarf delphiniums are great for cutting as their spikes are ideal for arranging and they don't teeter over. They require full sun, in a moist, humus-rich but well-drained soil. The Magic Fountains Series bloom in their first summer if you sow seed early indoors and plant them out after the last risk of frost. They may not be reliably upright in the first year, but from the second year on they are extremely sturdy and won't need staking.

Leucanthemum vulgare
'Maikönigin' (also known as 'May Queen')
Flowers: MAY–AUGUST
Height/spread: 50CM X 30CM
I love natural schemes, and this ox-eye daisy bridges the gap nicely between wild and cultivated. 'May Queen' produces early, single flowerheads on tall stems that are excellent for cutting and mixing with wildflowers on the windowsill. Grow in moderately fertile, moist, but well-drained soil in full sun or part-shade.

Lupinus 'Gallery Yellow'
and 'Gallery White'
Flowers: JUNE–JULY
Height/spread: 60CM X 40CM
Lupins are wonderful cottagey plants that offer so much colour, and the compact Gallery Series is perfect for growing in quantity for cutting. The handsome spikes look perfect in any number of different bouquet styles. Plunge cut stems into a bucket of water immediately. Blooms will start falling in about five days or earlier in a hot indoor location. Gallery Series lupins will bloom in just 15 or 16 weeks after a spring sowing. In subsequent years, each plant should produce up to a dozen, foot-long flower spikes. They will happily self-seed if you let them, too.

Dead-head cornflowers or shear back for another flush.

Rows make for easy picking and mean there's always space to sow more.

Your maintenance regime

You need constant vigilance and planning to grow a productive and diverse cutting garden. I haven't covered picking flowers – see page 198 for chapter and verse on that.

February

- Warm soil with fleece.
- Weed thoroughly, particularly fleshy-rooted perennial weeds, such as bindweed – forking to get as much of the root out of the soil as possible. Fast-growing weeds can out-compete your seedlings for light, water and nutrients.
- Order plug-grown annuals and chrysanthemums from specialists and seed suppliers.

March

- Rake a general fertiliser such as fish, blood and bone into the top 3cm of soil.
- Start off dahlias in pots of multi-purpose compost in a greenhouse, porch or coldframe.
- Plant half a dozen gladioli every few weeks from March until mid-summer and you'll have a constant supply of flowers until autumn.
- Direct-sow hardy annuals including nigella, cornflower and snapdragons.
- Sow sunflowers singly and sweet peas five to a 9cm pot on a windowsill or greenhouse.
- Sow zinnia, rudbeckia, moleucella, hordeum in pots or trays under glass.
- Sow lupins outdoors (or in autumn).
- Plant autumn-sown sweet peas and sow seeds direct in the soil for follow-on flowers.
- Be vigilant for slugs and snails and put out wildlife-friendly pellets or traps.

April
- Continue to direct-sow hardy annuals outdoors, including teasel and *Papaver somniferum*.
- Prick out seedlings grown indoors into individual 9cm pots and keep watered.
- Pot on chrysanths and plugs from seed suppliers into 9cm pots.
- Keep dahlias, plugs and seedlings watered in the greenhouse, bringing pots outside. on warm days from now until planting out to harden them off. Watch out for snails.
- Apply a high-potash liquid fertiliser to gladiolus when flower spikes reach half their final size. Repeat every fortnight until three weeks after flowering.
- Be vigilant for aphid attack from now on. Regular checking and pinching out tips of small. infestations is the key. If things get out of hand, spray with a mineral soap.

May
- Plant out chrysanths in soil improved with compost.
- Pot on young plants that are outgrowing their pots. Keep them well watered.
- Sow sunflowers outdoors or plant out earlier-sown, pot-grown plants.
- Sow molucella and zinnia in situ to follow on from those sown in pots.
- Plant annuals and dahlias outside once the last spring frosts have passed. Incorporate lots of compost into the planting hole.
- Dig up daffodils (with their leaves attached) and plant them elsewhere in the garden. Alternatively, leave them for six weeks and cut them to the ground.
- Stake tall or heavy-headed flowers and be quick to stand up any that get blown over.
- Keep annuals grown in rows neat and tidy with lengths of taught string tied to posts.
- Keep on top of watering from now on, especially in hot weather.

Collect seed from poppy pepper-pots in late summer.

June
- Plant the last of your gladioli bulbs early in the month for a final fling of autumn flowers.
- Plant out any remaining pot-grown flowers.
- Deadhead regularly.
- Pinch out the growing tips of chrysanthemums to encourage side-shoots of around three to four stems per plant.

July
- Order daffodil bulbs from specialist suppliers to get a choice pick.
- Trim the side-shoots from annuals and dahlias that are smothering their neighbours.
- Clear rows of spent blooms to make room for more pot-grown flowers, feeding the bare soil with bonemeal before planting.

August
- Pick and deadhead annuals to keep more flowers coming. Water rows if necessary.
- Shear back alchemilla to the crown for a fresh flush of growth. Water and feed with a balanced fertiliser and, if the weather is good, you'll get another show of flowers in September.
- Feed dahlias with a diluted liquid high-phosphate feed (tomato fertiliser) every week until early autumn. Also deadhead as the flowers fade.

September
- Sow hardy annuals in situ for early flowers next year.
- Collect seed from spent blooms for sowing next year. To collect snapdragon seeds, and guarantee new stock, allow the seedpods to dry on the plant and then break them open to gather the bounty.

October
- Sow sweet peas, five seeds to a 12cm pot and keep in a cold frame.
- Plant daffodil bulbs.
- Divide unproductive herbaceous residents while you can still identify them from their leaves.
- Lift gladioli corms when the leaves have turned brown in frost-prone areas. Dry them for a fortnight in a greenhouse and keep them in a dry, frost-free shed until spring.
- Lift and store dahlia tubers if your garden is cold or has very wet soil. Chop off the tops and pack in boxes of dry compost and keep in a shed. If you live in a warmer, drier area, chop them to the ground and cover them in a deep, dry mulch.

November–January
- Clear dead stems of annuals and cut back deciduous perennials to their crowns.
- Mulch the soil with a 4cm layer of garden compost.
- Plant tulips in November.

Dahlias and cosmos will fill vases
from July to the frosts.

Techniques for the Cut Flower Garden

Harvest regularly, as this is a form of advance deadheading which will keep the buds coming until autumn on annuals. Pick when flowers are just on the verge of opening for the longest-lasting, blooms and do it ideally in the cool of morning, putting stems straight into a bucket of water. Continue picking long-flowering annuals, including cosmos and sunflowers, and start picking first sprays of chrysanths by the end of September.

Roping back bushy plants

Staking is more important in part-shaded gardens as flowers lean towards the light and so are at risk of flopping. Stake clump-formers like asters with twiggy pea-sticks pushed in the soil around their crowns to hold them in place.

Support heavy spikes such as lupins by tying them individually to canes. With rows of bushy annuals like cosmos or cornflowers, create a corral by pushing two canes into the soil 25cm apart at the end of rows and looping twine around them 30 and 60cm above the ground. During the summer, trim off all wayward side-shoots before they crowd neighbours; it'll also encourage upright growth with longer, more versatile stems on your flowers.

How to plant gladioli bulbs in rows

Plant a gladioli every few weeks from March to July for a succession of cut flowers through summer into autumn. For the biggest flowers, fork well-rotted compost through the top soil before planting to hold moisture around their roots. For nice neat lines and efficient spacing use taut twine held between two pegs as a guide (1) and set out the gladioli corms 15cm apart leaving 45cm between the rows. Plant the corms 15cm deep – that's deeper than specified on their packets but this reduces their need for staking (3). Keep rows weeded (4), watered and fed with tomato fertiliser from when they run up to flower.

How to direct-sow hardy annuals in rows

Hardy annuals are child's play to grow as they come up quickly and flower for ages, if you deadhead them regularly. They also make wonderful cut flowers. Sow them in spring for summer blooms that are perfect for stuffing into a vase or giving as a gift. Sow taller plants in the centre of beds with shorter ones to the outside.

Choose a day when the weather is fine and the soil is moist but not waterlogged to sow your seeds. Preparation is key, so rake the soil to get rid of clods before sowing, discarding any large stones, with the aim of creating a crumbly chocolate tilth ideal for sowing into. Tread it flat to get rid of large air pockets.

You then need to enrich your soil a little. Annuals don't need masses of nutrients to grow well – in very rich soils, laced with barrow-loads of manure, they tend to gorge on plant food and become very tall and leafy but have little in the way of flower. Instead, use ordinary garden compost. This is enough to make the soil around the roots more moisture-retentive and will mean less watering for you. Rather than dig compost into the whole area, concentrate it along the rows, forking it into the surface along with a sprinkle of general fertiliser like fish, blood and bone.

If it's dry, remember to water with a rose on the watering can so you don't dislodge seeds and soil – seedlings should start to appear within a week to fourteen days. Young seedlings are very vulnerable to damage by slugs and snails, so employ whatever weapons you are prepared to use – I use wildlife-friendly slug pellets. They need topping up after rain and are less efficient than poisons, but at least you know children, pets and hedgehogs are safe. Toileting cats are the other danger, as they love to scratch the newly dug earth. The string lines along the rows tend to keep them away or, failing that, place peasticks at intervals over the beds.

Once the plants are up and growing, be sure to keep them watered if it's dry and pinch out tips when they're about 15cm high to make the plants bushy.

You will need:
Seeds | Labels | String | Bamboo canes
Watering can | Hoe | Rake

1: Stretch a length of string across prepared soil to act as sowing line (secure it with bamboo canes) and use a hoe to make a shallow drill. Create several drills in the same way, spacing them 50cm apart. Try and keep off the soil you are sowing into now.

2: Pour a can of water along the first drill and allow the moisture to drain away.

3: Sprinkle the seeds along the drill, spacing them roughly 5cm apart. If the seeds fall in a clump, use a finger to spread them out.

4: Cover the seed by gently brushing soil over the drill with your hands. Label the row and repeat until all the drills are sown.

Abundance and large leaves
make for a tropical effect.

11 | THE EXOTIC GARDEN

Whether you call it tropical, exotic or architectural, grouping together plants with large, lush foliage and zingy flowers makes a huge impact in a garden. It's a look first pioneered by the Victorians, who imported the style from the colonies, and I absolutely love it. The Exotic Garden at Greenacre has been a roaring success. It's in front of a heat-retaining, south-facing wall just next to the greenhouse, and there's easy access to a tap and waterbutt for the regular watering these thirsty plants need. The border is around 3 metres by 6 metres and transforms over the growing season from virtually nothing into a full-blown riot of flowers and foliage.

What I really enjoy about this style of growing is the sense of occasion. It's rather like preparing for a party. From winter until the frosts have finished in June, it's all about sowing, potting up and growing on in readiness for planting out and the fireworks ahead. All your efforts are rewarded ten times over, and from high summer until the first cold weather of autumn a tropical scheme gets better and better. If frosts come late you can even have the most amazing flowers in late autumn.

When frosts finally turn leaves to wilted flags, you have the satisfaction of putting the border to bed. Lift the most tender tubers and rhizomes, mulching the rest in readiness for winter. Leave the spikes and arching shapes of the hardy evergreens to carry on the show until spring, when the fun starts all over again.

In a nutshell: *this is a mix of exotic-looking hardy and tender plants which together look like they could be in the jungle. It peaks in summer and early autumn*

Suited to: *anyone who likes large-leaved exuberant schemes and hot colours*

Ideal location: *create a tropical scheme in front of a south-facing wall or in an extremely sheltered spot. You also need sun and rich, heavily-improved soil. A porch, shed or greenhouse is also a must*

Space needed: *you need a large area – at least 8 square metres*

Maintenance rating: *high. You'll need to be involved year round*

Eco credentials: *low. These plants and flowers aren't generally attractive to beneficial creatures*

1: *Melianthus major*

2: *Gladiolus* 'Zorro'

3: *Phormium* 'Sundowner'

4: *Tetrapanax papyrifer* 'Rex'

5: *Salvia* x *jamensis* 'Hot Lips'

6: *Gladiolus* 'Green Star'

7: *Ipomoea batatas* 'Blackie'

8: *Ensete ventricosum* 'Maurelii' or *Musa basjou*

9: *Dahlia* 'Magenta Star'

10: *Canna* 'Durban' or *Ricinus communis*

11: *Tithonia rotundifolia* 'Torch'

12: *Dahlia* 'Vuurvogel'

13: *Clematis* 'Rebecca'

14: *Trachycarpus fortunei*

15: *Fatsia japonica*

16: *Tigridia pavonia*

17: *Euphorbia* x *pasteurii*

18: Annual climbers

Exotic Garden elements

Size

Large-leaved plants like palms along with those that put on growth quickly are the key to a tropical scheme. Bananas, gingers, cannas all do the trick, along with many annual flowers and climbers.

Food

Tropical plants are hungry plants. To get the best from them, feed your soil with compost and well-rotted horse manure or a proprietary manure-based compost. In a new border, dig soil deeply, adding a barrow of manure to every two square metres.

Water

Tropical plants are also thirsty. Keep on top of watering, never letting soil dry out in summer. Install a waterbutt onto your guttering and save as much water as you can.

Support

Wire supports are essential to train climbers and help stake tall sail-like plants that grow fast and tend to get rocked by wind. Drill vine eyes into your wall or fence then string with plastic-covered garden wire.

Protection

Many exotic garden plants are tender and need winter protection. It's essential you keep on top of this as they're costly to replace if they succumb to frosty or wet conditions. You'll need somewhere frost-free, ideally a greenhouse, to store lifted, tubers and plenty of horticultural fleece.

Compost bin

You'll need lashings of mulch for any plants you leave in the ground.

Intermingle a variety of leaf shapes and shades for a luxuriant feel.

My plant choices

My selection is a mixture of hardy, architectural shrubs for year-round structure and come-and-go climbers, bulbs and annuals to give the scheme its tropical look. Large-leaved cannas, bananas and dahlias make up the height and bulk, while smaller annuals and climbers are used to bind the border together and cover the bare soil. Don't stint on these fillers even if they don't look as dramatic as the monster plants in the catalogue. Without them the border risks lacking cohesion and colour as the season progresses.

Annual climbers

Use to cover walls and to scramble through plants.

Cobaea scandens (AGM)

Flowers: JULY–OCTOBER

Height/spread: UP TO 10M

I always use the cup-and-saucer plant to create a tropical look quickly. It romps away producing masses of scrambling stems studded with creamy-green flowers, that age to a deep purple. Each resembles an upside-down cup and saucer, with a tangle of stamens in the centre. It's frost tender, although it will survive the winter on a warm wall in mild areas. Sow seed in spring, allowing one seed per 12cm pot. Harden off and plant out after the last spring frosts.

'The Cyprus vine
is unusual, with
fabulous branches
of bright green pinnate
leaves and bright red,
star-shaped tubular
flowers'

Ipomoea tricolor 'Heavenly Blue'

Flowers: JUNE–OCTOBER

Height/spread: 2M

Morning glory is a vigorous, twining annual with fragile-looking, funnel-shaped flowers. As well as 'Heavenly Blue' there are other colours – white, pale pink and purple. Although it looks strikingly similar to bindweed, don't worry, ipomoea is a completely different genus and totally frost tender. Soak seeds for 24 hours before sowing to encourage germination, and sow one seed per 9cm pot at 21°C. Provide plants with support and protect them from cold, drying winds.

Ipomoea quamoclit

Flowers: JUNE–OCTOBER

Height/spread: 5M

The Cyprus vine is unusual, with fabulous branches of bright-green pinnate leaves and bright red, star-shaped tubular flowers. It's native to tropical regions of northern South America and Mexico. It grows year round in the tropics and, like most tubular flowers, is pollinated by hummingbirds. Of course, it won't survive our temperate-zone winters, so use it as an annual like the regular morning glory.

Tropaeolum peregrinum

Flowers: JUNE–OCTOBER
Height/spread: 3.5M

The canary creeper at Greenacre reached the top of a 3m wall in the blink of an eye. It's a lovely, easy, but tender garden plant, not least for its extraordinary fringed blooms which look like tiny yellow birds flapping their wings. Sow seed indoors in pots in March, and then again in situ outdoors in May. This prevents early-sown plants running to seed if we have dry weather.

Evergreen structure

Vital for winter interest and for holding a scheme together. In cooler regions plants will be around two-thirds the given sizes, which are for the most sheltered spots.

Euphorbia x pasteurii

Flowers: MAY–JUNE
Height/spread: 2M X 2.5M

This tortoise-shaped evergreen is fast-growing and needs plenty of space to show off its full architectural effect. Stiff stems are clothed in narrow, dark green leaves, which have a distinctive cream go-faster strip central midrib. The stems are topped with clusters of honey-scented, yellowy-brown bracts followed by small seedpods that burst noisily on warm summer days. Grow in full sun or partial shade in a light, well-drained soil. Look out for and pot up seedlings in spring. Although hardy, young plants need winter protection in cold areas.

Fatsia japonica (AGM)

Flowers: SEPTEMBER–OCTOBER
Height/spread: 3M X 2M

Loved for its 'instant jungle' effect and easy-going nature, this hardy architectural behemoth has large, Bentley-green, leathery, palmate leaves that if well fed grow to 30cm or more across. Small creamy umbels of white flowers arrive in autumn, followed by clusters of black fruits. It's ideal for a shaded, sheltered courtyard, but also looks great in the Exotic Garden. Grow in fertile, moist but well-drained soil in full sun or light, dappled shade. Protect from cold, drying winds, which can turn shoots and leaves black. It's easy to propagate from greenwood cuttings in early or mid-summer.

'With its enormous leaves and umbels of autumn flowers, the rice-paper plant has to be one of the most exciting hardy exotic plants you can grow. It has all the drama of a Jurassic giant and then some.'

Melianthus major (AGM)

Flowers: MAY–JULY
Height/spread: 3M X 2M

The honey bush is an evergreen (or even everblue) shrub with huge, soft, but jagged-looking leaves and robust hollow stems. It needs protection from a south-facing wall, or a spot in a mild garden to flourish. Having said this, the melianthus at Greenacre was cut back to nothing after temperatures of -13°C in the winter of 2009/10 and has miraculously bounced back since. Grown in a moderately fertile, moist but well-drained soil in full sun it will produce aubergine-coloured flower spikes that last for months. Provide a dry winter mulch, protect from excessive winter wet and shelter from cold, drying winds.

Phormium 'Sundowner' (AGM)

Flowers: JULY
Height/spread: 2M X 2M

A good-natured and hardy tropical-looking plant that has broad and upright bronze-green leaves with rose-pink margins. Its sword-like stripes of colour provide a strong counterpoint among large, rounded green leaves. Grow in fertile, moist but well-drained soil in full sun. Provide a deep mulch in winter in frost-prone areas. If plants get too big you can divide in spring by lifting with a spade and splitting with a wood saw.

Tetrapanax papyrifer 'Rex'

Flowers: SEPTEMBER–OCTOBER
Height/spread: 3M X 3M

With its enormous leaves and umbels of autumn flowers, the rice-paper plant has to be one of the most exciting hardy exotic plants you can grow. It has all the drama of a Jurassic giant and then some. It's a thicket-forming evergreen shrub (or small tree) with stout shoots and leaves that are scaly on top and felted underneath. The one at Greenacre already looks very jungly, at just 2 metres high. In frost-prone areas, grow it against a warm wall or in a container that can be moved under cover in winter (see page xx). Grow in any well-drained soil in full sun, although give it shelter from strong winds.

Trachycarpus fortunei (AGM)

Flowers: JULY (although insignificant)
Height/spread: 10M X 3M

With the fur-like covering on its trunk and head of fan-shaped, dark green leaves you'd never imagine the Chusan palm is evergreen and hardy. It does best in shelter from strong winds, so its leaves don't get blown ragged, and likes well-drained, fertile soil in full sun. This palm does produce small, cup-shaped yellow flowers when mature, but it's the leaves that we all grow it for. It's also totally trouble-free and hardy.

The glorious 'African Queen' trumpet lily in July.

Giving *Clematis* 'Rebecca' a leg-up the furry trunk of *Trachycarpus fortunei*.

Frost-tender exotics

Grow for lush, tropical leaves.

Ensete ventricosum 'Maurelii'

Flowers: JUNE–AUGUST (if you're lucky)
Height/spread: 3M X 3M

Few tender plants fit in with a jungle scheme better than bananas. This ensete is very fast growing and produces huge olive-green, paddle-shaped leaves with splashes of red and a deep red midrib. Ensete thrive in a hot spot with free-draining, rich, well-watered soil. Plant out container-grown plants after the frosts then dig them up and keep in a frost-free place over winter – they're good houseplants if you have the room. *Musa basjoo* is a hardier but less ornamental plain green banana. In sheltered spots it can be overwintered outdoors if protected.

Ipomoea batatas 'Blackie'

Flowers: this plant is about foliage
Height/spread: 45CM X 45CM

This trailing foliage plant has heart-shaped, lobed, almost-black leaves. It's also known as the sweet potato vine and has trumpet-shaped purple blooms. I weave it around the feet of other plants in the Exotic Garden. It's a tender perennial so it won't survive frosty conditions. Grow in moderately fertile, well-drained soil in full sun and shelter from cold, drying winds. Sow seed in spring after chipping or soaking in water for 24 hours. Dig up the tubers at the end of the year and store like dahlias for planting next year.

Ricinus communis

Complements the colours in the exotic border and its foliage adds variety – see page 133 for details.

Jungle flowers

Grow for show-stopping colour and exotic blooms.

Canna 'Durban'

Flowers: JULY ONWARDS
Height/spread: 1.5M X 50CM

A red-leaved canna with yellow and pink tiger-striped leaves. See the Bedding Borders on page 131 for growing instructions .

Clematis 'Rebecca'

Flowers: JUNE–AUGUST
Height/spread: 2M X 2M

I trained this clematis up a trachycarpus at Greenacre, adding a bit of colour to the exotic palm. The flowers of this hybrid are large and a vivid, pillar-box red when they first emerge and they keep coming all summer. I planted it on the north side of the trachycarpus, so that the foliage and flowers naturally head up through the leaves towards the sunshine. It's planted a hand's width deeper than it was in the pot, to keep roots cool and to give it a fighting chance against the rare, but problematic, clematis wilt disease. Grow in fertile, humus-rich and well-drained soil in sun or a little shade.

Dahlia 'Magenta Star'

Flowers: JULY–OCTOBER

Height/spread: 1M X 80CM

Dahlias are perfect for a tropical border as they thrive in rich, moist soil in a sunny spot and have large, flamboyant flowers. 'Magenta Star' is a modern-looking single dahlia with flowers opening plum, paling to pink set off against carob-coloured leaves. Plant up tubers in a greenhouse or porch in March, then plant out after the frosts. Stake with peasticks to prevent the stems flopping. In mild areas and sandy soils, mulch in winter or in cold gardens lift tubers and store in compost-filled boxes in a shed.

Dahlia 'Vuurvogel'

Flowers: JULY–OCTOBER

Height/spread: 1M X 60CM

A cactus dahlia with an explosion of spiky pink and yellow petals that is 15cm wide. Staking is crucial as the flowers are so large and heavy. Grow as above.

Gladiolus 'Green Star' and 'Zorro'

Flowers: JULY–SEPTEMBER

Height/spread: 1M X 20CM

With their flamboyant, frilly blooms, gladioli might look exotic, but they're very easy to grow. 'Green Star' is one of the best green varieties, with flowers that remain fresh parakeet-green even as they mature. Dark-red 'Zorro' gives the tropical border real punch as the large red-velvet petals stand out brilliantly against the tropical foliage of its neighbours. Plant the corms in succession every few weeks, working backwards from when you want them to flower as they take around 100 days from when they first go in the ground. Water moderately as they grow. See page 199 for more details.

Lilium 'African Queen'

Flowers: JULY–AUGUST

Height/spread: 1.2M X 30CM

Scented apricot-coloured trumpets with a toffee-tinge top grace 1.2-metre stems. Plant the bulbs 15cm deep around evergreens so they come up through their leaves. Keep a beady eye out for the red lily beetles as their grubs chew the stems. If you spot any, pick them off and squash them.

Salvia x jamensis 'Hot Lips'

Flowers: OCTOBER

Height/spread: 50CM X 50CM

This bushy, low-growing tender sage has shapely lipstick-pink and white flowers in summer and autumn. Grow in light, humus-rich, moist and well-drained soil in full sun. Plants flourish on chalky or sandy soils but may not survive a cold winter, so take cuttings in autumn. We planted a drift in the tropical border. It's a bit of a chameleon as it produces all-red or all-white flowers in hot weather and returns to its normal bicolour state as the temperature dips in autumn.

Tigridia pavonia

Flowers: JULY–AUGUST
Height/spread: 1M X 15CM

The tiger flower is a striking plant that looks like an exotic jungle orchid. The red-speckled centre is framed by yellow bands with three distinctive orange petals radiating outwards, a bit like the mirrored view down a kaleidoscope tube. They're bulbous perennials from the sandy grasslands of Mexico and Guatemala but, because they're frost tender, we grow them as annuals. Plant 10cm deep in well-drained, sandy and fertile soil in full sun. If you want to keep yours over winter, lift bulbs after flowering and overwinter in dry sand at about 10°C.

Tithonia rotundifolia 'Torch'

Flowers: JULY–OCTOBER
Height/spread: 1.8M X 30CM

The tall, elegant Mexican sunflower has dahlia-like flowers in flamboyant shades of firework orange and red. We sow and grow them as annuals at Greenacre, and use them in both the Exotic Garden and The Bedding Borders. The warmth of our warm wall made all the difference to how well they performed, even in recent soggy summers.

Cactus-flower dahlias are perfect for exotic gardens.

Your maintenance regime

Tropical borders take effort and vigilance, but keep on top of these tasks and you'll be home and dry.

Spring
- Sow annuals (ipomoea, ricinus and tithonia, etc) at 21°C in the greenhouse, keeping them away from draughts. Grow them on at a minimum of 10°C.
- Stake annual climbers to prevent them becoming tangled in each other's stems. Pinching out also helps and makes them grow nice and bushy.
- Pot up dahlia tubers and canna rhizomes and keep them in a light, frost-free place.
- Pinch out dahlia tips to create bushy plants, and feed with fish, blood and bone.
- Protect any frost-prone plants in the border with a covering of fleece or hessian (see pages 218–19).

Late Spring
- Harden off seed-sown climbers and plants grown from tender tubers.
- Put wildlife-friendly slug pellets around new clematis shoots and other vulnerable plants.
- Give clematis a light prune, trimming out any of the dead or weak growth, then water and feed with a balanced fertiliser.
- Plant gladioli corms direct from March or April (as soon as the soil has warmed up a bit). Incorporate lots of manure when planting.

Early Summer
- Plant out dahlias, cannas and seed-sown tender plants after the last spring frosts have passed.
- Water all new plantings on a daily basis when it is dry.
- Stake dahlias to stop their stems snapping under heavy blooms later in the season.
- Prune evergreens to make space for flowers at ground level.

Summer
- Remove dead leaves from plants as they start to look tired.
- Feed trachycarpus and fatsia with a handful of high-nitrogen chicken manure once in June and again in July for green, healthy leaves.
- Watch out for cabbage white caterpillars on tropaeolum and act fast if you see any. Pick them off by hand or use a mineral soap spray.
- Apply a high-nitrogen liquid fertiliser monthly to the banana until late summer.
- Feed gladioli with a high-potash fertiliser every two weeks as they run up to flower.
- Feed dahlias weekly with a liquid fertiliser high in nitrogen and potash. If it's dry, water them at least once a week.
- Take semi-ripe tip cuttings of *Salvia* x *jamensis* 'Hot Lips' as insurance against winter losses (see page 73).

The fastest way to give hungry plants a boost is with a regular foliar feed.

Late Summer

- Feed plants with high-potash fertiliser to increase their hardiness.
- Deadhead dahlias and tithonia.
- Collect and store seed of annual climbers for sowing next spring.
- Foliar-feed flowers by wetting the leaves with a dilute high-potash tomato fertiliser to keep new buds coming into autumn (as shown above) and feed yellowing evergreens.
- Mulch gladioli corms to give them winter protection or dig up and store when the foliage has turned brown.

Autumn

- Dig up dahlia tubers as soon as leaves become frosted. Cut off the foliage, fork from the soil and keep them boxed up in dry multi-purpose compost in a frost-free shed for winte.r
- Lift canna rhizomes for winter storage, removing the stems and leaves. Cannas prefer to be kept in just-moist compost over winter and not allowed to dry out completely.
- Treat the black-leaved ipomoea like a canna – it can also be saved for next year.
- Protect tender plants that are in the ground by covering their roots with plastic topped with a layer of composted bark.
- Lift bananas before the first hard frosts and bring them indoors. Reduce top growth to the newest two or three leaves. Cut the dead leaves no lower than the base of each leaf blade.
- Remove suckers of tetrapanax to restrict its growth and stop it becoming thuggish.
- Cut back the faded flower stems of euphorbia, but remember to wear gloves and long sleeves, as the milky sap is poisonous and a skin irritant.
- Plant lilies 15cm deep in groups of three any time from now until sprin.g

Winter

- Mulch clematis in late winter with compost or well-rotted manure, avoiding the crown.
- Remove dead or yellowing foliage from cuttings and plants overwintered in the greenhouse to prevent mould spreading.
- In late winter, pot up cannas and dahlias.

Techniques for the Exotic Garden

Take cuttings for two reasons in an exotic border, firstly to bulk up on expensive plants cheaply, and secondly to create back-up for plants left outdoors in winter in case it's cold.

Bulking up and winter insurance

In March/April, once potted-up dahlia tubers have 12cm of growth, use a sharp knife to sever a stem just above the tuber (1). Take care not to damage the bud and tuber so it will re-shoot. Remove the bottom set of leaves (2), trim off snagged ends (3) dip the base of the cutting into rooting hormone and, using a dibber, push into pots of multi-purpose compost (4). Keep watered, warm and shaded in a covered propagator (or covered with a plastic bag) until the shoot starts to grow.

The Exotic Garden in winter

The trickiest part of looking after an exotic garden is knowing how and when to protect your precious plants when it gets cold. It's all about making the distinction between what can be left in the ground without being harmed, what can be left in but needs protecting, and what needs lifting and bringing under cover in winter. The lines get blurred by where you live in Britain, the local microclimate of your garden, how wet your soil gets in winter and how hard the cold hits in any given winter. Hardiness is not an exact science; young plants are less hardy than more mature ones, as are plants in wet clay soils.

Leave in situ

Hardy, leave in situ: of my selection, only the clematis and the plants listed as 'evergreen structure' can be left confidently in the border through winter. Phormium and clematis are reliably hardy and don't need winter protection.

Hardy but protect from scorched leaves in first year or in very cold periods: fatsia, euphorbia and trachycarpus are pretty tough, but may need covering with fleece if it's very cold in their first year. If you live in a city or plants are next to a warm wall in a sheltered garden you increase their chances of survival.

Tender, leave in situ but wrap in fleece or hessian: tetrapanax and *Musa basjoo* should be wrapped with hessian or fleece once frosts start to hit, and it should be left on for the duration of winter until early March. But if it gets cold again use a temporary cover (see project on pages 218–18).

Lift and replant

Lift or mulch: gladioli corms and the rhizomes of *Ipomoea* 'Blackie' and canna lilies should be lifted and brought into a frost-free place as soon as the frosts hit. They're not as tough as dahlias and tigridia, which can survive in mild winters and soils that don't get too wet in winter with a 5cm layer of mulch. Do lift dahlias in cold gardens. Ensete should be lifted and grown in a pot in the greenhouse, frost-free porch or conservatory.

Resow every spring: though some may self-seed, the intention with the annuals and annual climbers is that they are re-sown each spring. A cobaea I grew on a sheltered south-facing wall in Cambridge city centre survived for many winters with merely a spring prune to tidy up the straggly stems. Its seeds even used to germinate in the sand beneath the decking at its feet. Eventually it succumbed one cold winter, but fortunately all are so fast-growing that a spring sowing means you have flowering growth the same summer.

Take cuttings: *Salvia* x *jamensis* might come through a mild winter but it is always safer to take cuttings in summer. These should be grown in a greenhouse in winter and planted back out in the border after the frosts finish.

How to protect tender plants from frosts

Wherever you live in the UK there's always the risk that unexpected frosts will damage plants, both in spring when newly planted annuals, cuttings-grown plants, dahlias and cannas can be killed or set back, or in autumn when an early frost can put a premature end to your prize canna or tihtonia which could have otherwise given another month of loveliness before the next frost. The solution is to keep a beady eye on weather forecasts at these changeable times of year and dash out with the fleece before nightfall. That's why I have devised a system that allows plants to be covered quickly at Greenacre, a shelter made from timber posts and cords that support horticultural fleece or hessian held in place with clothes pegs. It might not look substantial, but it makes all the difference when it comes to stopping frost falling on leaves and flowers and blackening them. The posts stay in the soil, ideally hidden as much as possible by the leafy jungliness, until all danger has passed or what you've been protecting has been lifted for winter.

You will need:
2 timber posts | 4 vine eyes | Sash cord | 1 roll of 1.5m fleece or hessian | 20 wooden clothes pegs | Lump hammer | Drill

1: Hammer the posts into the soil at the front of the border either side of the plants you want to protect – ideally they should be above the tops of the foliage.

2: Screw vine eyes into the top of the posts and at a similar height on the wall behind.

3: String sash cord between the vine eyes and gently pull taut.

4: Drape fleece or hessian over the cords and posts and clip it in place with clothes pegs.

How to check for life after winter

The question on every gardener's lips after a hard winter is, 'Is it dead?' and the way to find out before you dig up a shrub or woody perennial and put it on the compost heap is with the scrape test. With a sharp knife, scrape away a small section of outer bark low on the plant's stem. If it's green, it's alive, if it's brown, scrape again lower by the roots. If it's alive, wait for the plant to reshoot from the base so you can clearly see and prune out what is dead.

1

2

3

4

Note: page numbers in **bold** refer to photographs and illustrations.

Acanthus mollis **184**, 190
Alchemilla 27, 119, 196
  A. mollis 105, **106**, 113, **185**, 190
Allium 45, 64–w5, 87, 144
  A. christophii 65, **65**
  A. 'Globemaster' **37**, 64, **64**
  A. hollandicum 'Purple
  Sensation' 64
  A. 'Mont Blanc' 47, **47**
  A. schubertii 64
  A. sphaerocephalon **32**, 62,
  65, **65**
  A. stipitatum 'Mount
  Everest' 42, 49
alpines 56
Ammi majus 53, 173, 174, **174**
Anemanthele lessoniana 154
Anemone 57
  A. nemorosa **106**, 109, 119
  A. x hybrid **106**, 114
Angelica archangelica **62**,
  65–6, **65**
annuals 13, 46–7, 94, 171–2,
  181, 184, 186–9, 194–6, 200,
  201, 206–7
Anthemis 86
  A. tinctoria **79**, 80, **81**
Antirrhinum **39**, 45, 53, 194,
  196
  A. majus 46, **185**, 186
aphids 35, 55
archways 78
Armeria maritima 162
Artemisia 55, 100
  A. 'Powis Castle' **44**, 50, **94**,
  96, 102
Asparagus officinalis 190
aspect 16
Astelia 55
  A. chathamica **44**, 50–1
Aster 30, 141, **149**, 150, 152–3
  A. lateriflorus 'Lady in
  Black' **62**, 66
  A. 'Little Carlow' 142, 144–5,
  144, 147
Astrantia 80, 86
  A. 'Hadspen Blood' **37**, **79**,
  80, **80**
  A. major **79**, 80–2
Atriplex hortensis var.
  rubra 173, 174, 177

bamboo 105, 107, **108**, 109,
  118–19
banana 24, 130, 135, 206,
  214–15
Bank 8, 93–123, **94–5**
bare-root plants 19
Bedding Border 9, 125–39,
  126–7
Bee Border 9, 61–75, **62**
bee boxes 63, 74, **75**
beech 61
bees **38**, 60, 61–75, 173
biennials 13, 45–7
birds 35
Bouteloua gracilis **142**, 148,
  154
bulbs 15, 45–50, 109–13, 144,
  189–90

Calamagrostis 150
  C. x acutiflora 'Karl
  Foerster' **142**, 149, **149**
Calibrachoa **88**, 89
Camellia 119
  C. x vernalis 'Yuletide' **107**,
  114
Canna 24, 130, **134**, 135–6,
  206, 214–15, 217–18
  C. 'Black Knight' **127**, 131
  C. 'Durban' **204**, 211
  C. 'Wyoming' **127**, 131, **131**
Carex 'Amazon Mist' **106**,
  115
caterpillars 35, 58
Centaurea cyanus **174**, 174
  C. c. 'Black Boy' **184**, 186, **186**
Centranthus ruber 'Albus'
  158, 162–3, **162**
Chaenomeles speciosa
  'Nivalis' 113
Chrysanthemum 35, **185**, 195,
  196, 198
  C. 'Beppie Red' **18**, **185**, 192
  C. 'Energy' **185**, 192
  C. 'Orange Allouise' **185**, 192,
  192
cineraria 100, 102, 126
Cirsium rivulare
  'Atropurpureum' **62**, 66,
  66, 72
Cistus 100
  C. x purpureus 'Alan Fradd'

94, 98
Clarkia amoena 174
Clematis 19, 24, 35, 86, 214, 217
  C. 'Elizabeth' **106**, 117, 119
  C. 'Rebecca' **204**, **210**, 211, **211**
  C. tangutica **106**, 117, 119
  C. x triternata 84, 177
Cleome hassleriana 'Helen
Campbell' 46
climbers 84–5, 117, 206–7
Coastal Garden 8, 157–69,
  158–9
Cobaea 217
  C. scandens 206
cobblestones 90, **91**
coleus 126
Colocasia 24, 130, 135–6
  C. esculenta **127**, 131–2
colour schemes 126
  purple-blue *see* Bee Border
  white *see* Twilight Garden
compost 16, 205
Consolida ajacis 175
containers 14, 78
contrast 14–15, 45–6
coppicing 100
Coreopsis 179
  C. tinctoria 173, **175**, 175
corms 109–13, 189–90
cornflower 170, 173, 194, 198
Cosmos 45, 46, 173, 179, **182**,
  198
  C. bipinnatus 46, **46**, 175, **175**,
  185, 186
cottage-gardens *see*
Scented Front Garden
cotton lavender 29, 167
Crambe 57, 160
  C. maritima **158**, 163, **163**
Cut Flower Garden 9,
  183–201, **184–5**
cutting back 27, 120, **120**, 152
cuttings 55, 100, 216–17
  basal 55, 150, 152, **153**
  root 57, 166
  summer stem 72–3, 166, 167
Cyclamen hederifolium
  106, 110
Cynara 55
  C. cardunculus **44**, 51, 51
Cytisus 86
  C. battandieri **79**, 84

daffodil *see* narcissus
Dahlia 24, 35, 46, 55, 136, 184, 184, 194–6, 206, 214–18
 D. 'Joe Swift' **44**, 51–2
 D. 'Magenta Star' **15**, **204**, 212, **213**
 D. 'Rothesay Reveller' **20**, 182, 184, 189
 D. 'Twyning's After Eight' **44**, 52, **52**
 D. 'Vuurvogel' **204**, 212, **212**
Daphne bholua 'Jacqueline Postill' **62**, 66
daylily 141
deadheading 13, 27, 55
Delphinium 30, 185
 D. 'Magic Fountains Dark Blue with White Bee' **184**, 193
Dianthus 86
 D. 'Mrs Sinkins' **79**, 82
Dicentra 57
 D. spectabilis **104**, **106**, 113
Digitalis 45, 55, 118–19
 D. purpurea 44, 47, **106**, 113, 116
Dipsacus fullonum **185**, 186
diseases 120, 136
division 33, 118, 150, 155
drought-tolerance 89, 93, 160

earwigs 35
Echinacea 57, 141, 150, 151, 153
 E. purpurea 'Rubinstern' **25**, **142**, **145**, 145
 E. 'Summer Sky' **152**
Echinops 150
 E. bannaticus 'Taplow Blue' **62**, 66
 E. ritro 'Veitch's Blue' **142**, 145
Echium 72
 E. candicans **62**, 68
 E. vulgare **62**, 68
Elaeagnus 86, 89
 E. 'Quicksilver' **79**, 85
Elymus 160
 E. hispidus 88, 89, **158**, 162
Ensete 136, 139
 E. ventricosum 'Maurelii' **127**, 132, **204**, 209
Erigeron 56, 156
 E. karvinskianus 24, **158**, 163,

163
Eryngium 55, 57, 160, 166
 E. bourgatii 'Picos Amethyst' **44**, 51
 E. giganteum **158**, 163–4, **163**
 E. pandanifolium **158**, 164
Erysimum 72, 73
 E. 'Bowles's Mauve' **62**, 68
 E. cheiri 'Blood Red' 129
Eschscholzia californica 93, **94**, **97**, 99, 101–2, 176
Eupatorium 149
 E. purpureum 142, 145, **145**
Euphorbia 80, 125, 135–6, 215, 217
 E. myrsinites **158**, 160, 167
 E. polychroma 129–30, **129**
 E. x *pasteurii* **204**, 207
evergreens 46, 105, 107, 160, 207–8
Exotic Garden 9, 203–19, **204**

Fargesia rufa **106**, 109
Fatsia 214, 217
 F. japonica **204**, 207
feeding 16, 24, 86, 205
fences 122, 122–3
flowering times 13
flowerlessness 36
Foeniculum vulgare 76, 86, 87
 F. v. 'Purpureum' **79**, 80, 82, **85**
foliage 126
foxglove *see* Digitalis
Front Garden, Scented 8, 77–91, **79**

gabions 159, 169
Galanthus nivalis **102**, 110, **110**, 118
gazania 130
Genista 100
 G. aetnensis **94**, 98
Gentiana '*Blue Silk*' **106**, 115
Geranium
 cranesbills 27, 68, **68**
 G. renardii **79**, 82
 G. 'Rozanne' **62**, 68, **68**
Gladiolus **185**, 194, 196, 199, **199**, 214–15, 217
 G. 'Black Star' **185**, 189–90

 G. 'Green Star' **204**, 212
 G. nanus **28**, 190–1
 G. 'Zoro' **204**, 212
Glaucium flavum f. *fulvum* **158**, 164
godetia 170
golden hop 119
grasses 148–50, 154–5, 160

Halimium lasianthum **94**, 98
hardening off 138
hardiness 14
hawthorn 59
hazel panels 122, **122**–3
height 14, 78, 126, 143, 159
Helenium 27, 150–3
 H. autumnale **62**, 68
 H. 'Sahin's Early Flowerer' **142**, 146
Helianthus 150
 H. annuus **185**, 187, **187**
 H. 'Lemon Queen' **142**, 146, **146**
Helichrysum **94**, 100
 H. italicum **94**, 96, 102
Helleborus 105, 112, 118–20, 120
 H. foetidus **106**, 115
 H. x *hybridus* **106**, 115, **115**
Hesperis 55
 H. matronalis **44**, 47
Heuchera 105, 107, 118
 H. 'Beaujolais' **106**, 117
 H. 'Purple Petticoats' **106**, 117
hoeing 23
Hordeum 194
 H. jubatum 33, 182, **185**, 187, **187**
Hosta 'Sum and Substance' **106**, 114
Humulus lupulus 'Aureus' **107**, 117

Indocalamus latifolius **106**, 109
Ipomoea 215
 I. batatas 'Blackie' 126, **204**, 211, 217
 I. quamoclit 206–7
 I. tricolour 'Heavenly Blue' 206, **206**

Note: page numbers in **bold** refer to photographs and illustrations.

ironwork railings 78
ivy 126

Knautia macedonica **62**, 68–9, **68**

ladybirds 36
lady's mantle *see*
Alchemilla mollis
Lampranthus **158**, 166–7, **166**
landscape materials 108
larkspur 173
Lathyrus odoratus **184**, 194, 196
   L. o. 'Albutt Blue' **184**, 188, **188**
Lavandula 27, **32**, 55, 72–3, 94, 100, **185**
   L. angustifolia 'Munstead' **94**, 96, 102
   L. stoechas 44, 52, **94**, 96, 102
   L. x chaytoriae 'Sawyers' 61, **62**, 69, **69**
'layer' planting 105
Leucanthemum vulgare 193
life, testing for 218, **218**
lifting plants 33
Lilium **76**, 87, 215
   L. 'African Queen' **209**, 212
   L. regale **44**, 49
Limonium platyphyllum **158**, 164
Linaria 177
   L. maroccana 176
Linum grandiflorum 'Rubrum' 176
Lonicera periclymenum 'Graham Thomas' 79, 85
Lupinus 184, **185**, 193, 194, 198
Lychnis 55, 87
   L. coronaria 'Alba' **44**, 79, 82

maintenance 23–33, 55, 72, 86–7, 100, 118–19, 135–6, 150–1, 166, 179, 194–6, 214–15
mammals 36
manure 16, 24
   green 95, 101
Melianthus major **204**, 208
midden piles 167
Miscanthus 150
   M. sinensis **142**, 148–9, 154

Moluccella laevis 188, 194–5
Monarda 72
   M. 'Fishes' **62**, 69
moths 43, 58–9
Muehlenbeckia complexa 126, 132–3, 135–6
mulch 16, 95, 106–7, 205
Musa basjoo 217
mycorrhizae 19

Narcissus 45, **106**, 110, **111**, 118–19, 190, 195–6
   N. 'Actaea' 110
   N. 'Cheerfulness' 110
   N. 'Dutch Master' 110
   N. 'Jonquilla' 110–12
   N. 'Minnow' 112
   N. poeticus var. recurvus 112
   N. 'Quail' 112
   N. 'Rijnvelds Early Sensation' 112
   N. 'Spellbinder' 112
   N. 'TRENA' 113
Nectaroscordium siculum **119**, 144
nematodes 36
Nemesia 88, **89**
Nepeta 27, 72
   N. 'Six Hills Giant' **62**, 69
Nicotiana 30, **39**, 45, 46
   N. sylvestris **44**, 47
Nigella 173, 194
   N. damascena 176, **185**, 189

pacelia 173
Panicum 150
   P. virgatum 'Heavy Metal' **142**, 148
Papaver **94**
   P. commutatum 176
   P. orientale 27
   P. rhoeas 176, **176–7**
   P. somniferum **185**, 189, 195
Parthenocissus henryana **107**, 117
Passiflora 55
   P. caerulea **44**, 52
pathways 78, 90, **91**, 121
pebbles 158
Pelargonium sidoides 88, **89**
Pennisetum **132**, 134, 136, 150, 151

   P. alopecuroides 'Hameln' 148
   P. setaceum **127**, 133, 136
   P. villosum 154
peony 27, 30
perennials 13, 33, 50–2, 80–3, 113–17, 144–8, 162–4, 186–9, 190–3
Persicaria
   P. amplexicaulis 'Firedance' **142**, 146
   P. rosea **147**
pests 35–6, 55, 72, 179
Phacelia **170**
   P. tanacetifolia 99, 173
Phlox paniculata 'Mount Fuji' 52–3, 79, **82**
Phormium 29, 217
   P. 'Sundowner' **158**, 160, **204**, 208
Phyllostachys
   P. aureosulcata **107**, 109
   P. bissetii **107**, 109
pinching out 152
plant invigorators 24, 35
planting distance 17
planting tips 17–19
Polemonium caeruleum **62**, 69
Polystichum setiferum 'Herrenhausen' 113
poppy 166, 170, 173, **182**
   see also Eschscholzia californica; Papaver
pot marigold 102
pot-bound plants 18
Prairie Border **9**, 141–55, **142**
propagation 143, 154–5
   see also cuttings; division
protection 205, 217–18, **219**
pruning 13, 27, 55, 100
Pulmonaria 38
   P. 'Blue Ensign' **14**, **62**, 69–70
purple orache 85

repetition 126
Ricinus communis **127**, 133, 133–4, 135–6, 211
rock gardens *see* Coastal Garden
Rosa 14, 24, 43, 55, 77, 80, 83–4, 86–7
   Kew Gardens **44**, 52

maintenance 55
planting 18–19
pruning 27
R. 'Gertrude Jekyll' **79**, 83
R. 'Strawberry Hill' **79**, 83, 84, **84**
row planting 95, 102, **103**, 185
Rudbeckia 153, 194
R. fulgida var. *deamii* **142**, 146
R. hirta 'Cherry Brandy' **185**, 189

Salix exigua **94**, 99–100
Salvia 27
S. nemerosa 'Caradonna' **62**, 70, **70**
S. x *jamensis* 'Hot Lips' **204**, 212, 214, 217
Sambucus 55
S. nigra f. *porphyrophylla* 'Eva' 44, 46, 52, **79**, 84, **84**, 86
Santolina 166
S. chamaecyparissus **158**, 160
sawfly 35
scale insects 35
Scented Front Garden 8, 77–91, **79**
screens 78
sea holly *see Eryngium*
sea lavender 166
seathrift 160
second-flushes 27
sedge 107, 118–19
Sedum 150, 153
S. 'Herbstfreude' **142**, 148
S. 'Little Cauli' **143**
S. 'Red Cauli' **142**, 148
S. spectabile **62**, 70
seed
collecting/storing 180, **180**, 196
sowing 101, **101**, 154, 181, **181**, 200, **201**
Seed-packet Meadow 9, 171–81, **172–3**
self-seeders 160
sempervivum 56
Senecio cineraria 'Silver Dust' 96
shady schemes *see* Woodland Garden

shape 13–14
shelter 16, 45, 63
shrubs 50–2, 84–5, 94, 98–9, 113–17
moving 139, **139**
site preparation 15–16
sloping plots *see* Bank
slugs 36
smoke bush 80
snails 36
snapdragon *see Antirrhinum*
snowdrop *see Galanthus nivalis*
soil 13, 15–16, 93, 106, 143, 157, 171, 181
soil improvers 16, 24, 95, 106–7
spider mite 35
squirrel-tail grass *see Hordeum jubatum*
Stachys byzantina **79**, 83
Stipa **29**, 166
S. tenuissima 154, **158**, 162, **162**
structure 168–9
succulents 56
sun plants 16, 143
sunflower 173, 194, 195, 198
support 30, 198, 205
sweet pea *see Lathyrus odoratus*
sweet rocket 45

Tanacetum 72
t. coccineum **62**, 70
teasel 195
tender plants 14, 217–18
Tetrapanax 215, 217
T. papyrifer 'Rex' **204**, 208
Teucrium 100
T. fruticans **94**, 98, 102
texture 143
thrift 169
Tigridia 217
T. pavonia **204**, 213, **213**
timbers 159, 168
Tithonia 130, 135, 214, 218
T. rotundifolia 'Torch' **127**, 133, **204**, 213
Trachycarpus 214, 217
T. fortunei **204**, 208, **210**
Tradescantia 135–6

T. pallida **127**, 133
tree canopy 106–7
Trifolium rubens **62**, 70–1
Tropaeolum 214
T. peregrinum 207, **207**
tubers 189–90
Tulipa 45, 49–50, 55, 87, 124, 125, **128**, 135, 136, 196
lifting/storing 49, 55, 137, **137**
T. 'Ballerina' **22**, 129, 130, **130**
T. 'Barcelona' 129, 130, **130**
T. 'Maureen' 49
T. 'Purissima' 49
T. 'Rem's Favourite' 49, **49**
T. 'Spring Green' **48**, 49
T. 'Swan Wings' 49
T. 'White Dream' 50
T. 'White Marvel' 50
T. 'White Triumphator' **21**, 50
Twilight Garden 9, 43–59, **44**

Uncinia rubra 115

valerian 169
Verbascum **29**
V. bombyciferum **158**, 164
Verbena
V. bonariensis **94**, 99, **99**, 102
V. rigida **62**, 71, 72
Veronicastrum virginicum 'Erica' **62**, 71
vine eyes and wires 78
vine weevils 36

wallflower 125, 135
walls, planting 56
waterbutts 78
watering 23, 205
weed-suppressing membranes 158
weedkillers 23
weeds 17, 23, 167, 179, 194
whitefly 35
wildlife 173
see also Bee Border
windowboxes 78, **88**, 89
Woodland Garden 9, 105–23, **106–7**

Zinnia 194, 195
Z. elegans **185**, 189

ACKNOWLEDGEMENTS

This book would not have been possible without the help and hard work of the Gardeners' World production team, in particular gardeners Ned Harvey and Joe Hodge. Jason Ingram as always has been a pleasure to work with, as have Caroline McArthur, Lorna Russell and Kevin Smith. I'd also like to thank Lisa for her support, Scott Jessop for his wonderful illustrations, David Eldridge and Dom Cooper for their design, Antony Heller for production, and Dr Zoe Randle from Moths Count.

This book is published to accompany the television series entitled *Gardeners' World*.
Executive Producer: Gill Tierney | Series Producer: Liz Rumbold

Published in 2011 by BBC Books, an imprint of Ebury Publishing. A Random House Group Company
Copyright © Toby Buckland 2011 | Photography © Jason Ingram 2011 Jason Ingram is an award-winning garden photographer whose work appears in countless books and magazines. He has worked on *Gardener's World* providing publicity shots and stills for *Gardeners' World Magazine* for 7 years. | Illustrations © Scott Jessop 2011 | Toby Buckland has asserted his right to be identified as the author of this Work in accordance with the Copyright, Designs and Patents Act 1988 | All rights reserved. No part of this publication may be reproduced, stored in a retrieval system, or transmitted in any form or by any means, electronic, mechanical, photocopying, recording or otherwise, without the prior permission of the copyright owner.

The Random House Group Limited Reg. No. 954009 | Addresses for companies within the Random House Group can be found at www.randomhouse.co.uk | A CIP catalogue record for this book is available from the British Library | ISBN 978 1 84 607865 1

The Random House Group Limited supports the Forest Stewardship Council (FSC), the leading international forest certification organisation. All our titles that are printed on Greenpeace approved FSC certified paper carry the FSC logo. Our paper procurement policy can be found at www.rbooks.co.uk/environment

FSC
www.fsc.org
MIX
Paper from
responsible sources
FSC™ C004592

Commissioning editor: Lorna Russell | Project editor: Caroline McArthur | Copy-editor: Kevin Smith
Designer: TwoAssociates | Illustrations: Scott Jessop | Photographer: Jason Ingram | Production: Antony Heller |
Colour origination: XY Digital | Printed and bound in Germany by Firmengruppe APPL, Wemding
To buy books by your favourite authors and register for offers, visit www.rbooks.co.uk